The Diary of John Comer.

THE DIARY OF JOHN COMER.

EDITED WITH NOTES BY
C. EDWIN BARROWS, D. D.,
Late Pastor of First Baptist Church, Newport, R. I.

WITH AN INTRODUCTION AND A FEW ADDITIONAL NOTES BY
JAMES W. WILLMARTH, D. D., L.L.D.,
Pastor of Roxborough Baptist Church, Philadelphia

VOLUME VIII.
IN THE COLLECTIONS OF THE
RHODE ISLAND HISTORICAL SOCIETY.

PUBLISHED FOR THE SOCIETY
1893.

he Baptist Standard Bearer, Inc.

NUMBER ONE IRON OAKS DRIVE • PARIS, ARKANSAS 72855

Thou hast given a *standard* to them that fear thee;
that it may be displayed because of the truth.
-- Psalm 60:4

*Reprinted
by*

THE BAPTIST STANDARD BEARER, INC.
No. 1 Iron Oaks Drive
Paris, Arkansas 72855
(479) 963-3831

THE WALDENSIAN EMBLEM
lux lucet in tenebris
"The Light Shineth in the Darkness"

ISBN #1-57978-028-8

DEDICATION.

THE EDITOR

IS PERMITTED TO INSCRIBE THIS VOLUME

TO ONE

WHOSE PRESENCE, DURING HER LIFE, WAS A CONSTANT INSPIRATION
AND THE MEMORY OF WHOM, NOW THAT SHE HAS
DEPARTED, SHALL BE A PERPETUAL
INCENTIVE TO HIGHER
SERVICE.

TABLE OF CONTENTS

Complete Title..page 1

Baptist Standard Bearer Logo..............................page 2

Dedication..page 3

Table of Contents...page 4

Prefatory Note...page 5

Introduction..page 7

Inscription..page 14

Main Text of the Book......................................page 15

Index to Diary...page 127

Index to Footnotes...page 130

About the Author...page 133

PREFATORY NOTE.

THIS work, believed to be of historical interest and value to the general public, to the citizens of Rhode Island, and to the Baptist Denomination, is published by the American Baptist Publication Society in conjunction with the Rhode Island Historical Society, for which it was originally edited and annotated. A portion of the first edition bears the imprint of the latter Society.

The stereotype plates are provided by the generosity of Hon. Horatio Gates Jones, of Philadelphia, and Mr. Samuel A. Crozer, of Upland, Penna.

The autograph of John Comer is given on page 15, and was furnished by the kindness of Hon. H. G. Jones.

For a statement explanatory of the Dedication of this volume, *see* Introduction, page 12.

It will be understood, of course, that responsibility for opinions expressed in the Notes and Introduction belongs entirely to the writers.

J. W. W.

ROXBOROUGH, PHILADELPHIA, Oct. 15, 1892.

INTRODUCTION.

JOHN COMER was born in Boston, Mass., August 1, 1704. He pursued his perparatory studies at Cambridge, with a view of entering Harvard College, where he became a member of a Congregational church; but entered Yale College instead of Harvard in September, 1722. After a time, embracing Baptist sentiments, he was baptized January 31, 1725, becoming a member of the First Baptist Church, in Boston. He did not complete his course at Yale, but after his baptism began to preach. He spent a short time in Swanzey, Mass., teaching school and preaching, and in November, 1725, entered on his ministry in Newport, R. I., at the early age of twenty-one. Here he spent about six years, first as co-pastor of the First Baptist Church with Elder Wm. Peckham, and afterward, as what would probably now be called "stated supply" (in part, for there was another minister,) of the Second Baptist Church. His work at Newport was faithfully done, and was productive of great good; but erelong he found himself beset by many embarrassments. His doctrinal sentiments were Calvinistic, and he soon came to be a firm believer in the practice of "laying on of hands" upon newly baptized believers. The First Church was Calvinistic, but it resisted his attempt to introduce the strict observance of the "laying on of hands." It ought to be remembered that Mr. Comer's opinion was not an idiosyncrasy. Great numbers of Baptists in the seventeenth century, probably the large majority of them, believed this usage to be scriptural and obligatory. The same view was widely held in the eighteenth century. Mr. Comer's resignation resulted from this controversy. With the Second Church he was in harmony on this point; but they were Arminians in doctrine, and did not relish the preaching of the "doctrines of grace." All these difficulties, during which Mr. Comer seems to have exhibited a firm regard for what he believed to be the truth, tempered by a kind and Christian spirit, are set forth in his Diary. Isaac Backus describes him as "an excellent preacher of the gospel," and says that he was 'an eminent instrument of reviving doctrinal and practical religion in Newport." In 1731 he removed to Rehoboth, Mass. A Baptist church was formed there which was in accord with his views of truth and order, and in less than two years it increased to a membership of ninety-five. While in Newport he had occasionally done missionary work; now he labored not only at home but in Sutton, Leicester, Middleborough, and other places. A bright future seemed to be before him. His ability, piety, and wisdom marked him out for high usefulness and leadership among the New England Baptists, who were then a "feeble folk," struggling with opposition and persecution. But in his zeal he taxed his physical powers too severely, contracted consumption, and "died joyfully" at Rehoboth, May 23, 1734, when not yet quite thirty years of age.

His DIARY, covering the greater part of his life, is of an antique pattern. He often jots down occurrences in the fewest possible words. He deals little with the pictorial and picturesque elements. He reveals himself as a man of thought, of decision, and of piety; but his expressions often appear to us quaint; his reflections, always pervaded by a devout spirit, seem occasionally childlike, especially in the religious awe awakened by every unusual phenomenon or striking event. It was the way of the times to regard every calamity as a judgment, and to look upon many natural phenomena with fear, as portents of wrath, rather than with scientific inquiry and with admiration of God's wonderful displays of his power. This was no doubt an error. Yet who shall say that John Comer was not right in his unquestioning belief in God's providential control of the world, and that his mental attitude was not far nearer the right than the less believing and more flippant temper of this generation? Surely, we may learn something of wisdom and reverence from men like him, even if their quaintness and simplicity sometimes create a smile. When too, we consider the youth of the writer, I think we shall be impressed with the feeling that he was a man of strong intellect and noble powers, and that only his early death prevented him from becoming a commanding figure in the history of his people and in the literature of his day.

As we read this old-fashioned Diary we are carried back to days that, in some respects, seem to belong to remote antiquity For, two hundred years ago there was not a railroad or steamboat or telegraph or telephone in the world. Men traveled and communicated with each other in the most primitive ways. This country was new, sparsely settled, undeveloped, and bound by ties of political and commercial dependence to the mother country beyond the sea, to cross which was a far more formidable undertaking than it is now to circumnavigate

INTRODUCTION.   9

the globe. Life flowed on in a moderate current, with a slowness which to us would perhaps be intolerable. Questions of public policy, of international relations, of theological thought were all widely different in form, if not in substance, from those that agitate our minds. Many truths and facts, especially of science, now familiar as the alphabet, were then wholly unknown; and many old beliefs and superstitions, now vanished, held full sway or lingered in many minds. Projects now successfully accomplished or hopefully entertained, would then have seemed the wildest vagaries; and some matters then of grave concern, would now have no interest. Was this life, therefore, radically different from ours? Do its simple and quaint annals possess no charm for us and convey no lessons for our instruction? Whoever attentively reads this Diary will experience, first, an impression of freshness and strangeness, as if he had had a glimpse of a world almost unknown. But, presently, he will see the unchangeable elements and principles of human nature and of God's grace at work in that simple state of society. He will perceive that piety, bravery, truth, and honor have all times as their own; and he will not refuse to receive some precious lessons from the Diary of honest John Comer.

Certainly, historically considered, this Diary, which is often quoted by Backus and others, is valuable. The church historian, desirous of understanding the doctrines and practices of that early day, and of rescuing from oblivion a multitude of interesting and instructive facts, will find in it much material. The secular historian, especially in the line of local history, will also find here memoranda of events, accounts of curious circumstances, details concerning men and things, which will aid him in his researches, and throw a good deal of light upon the conditions of life and of thought almost two hundred years ago. Every citizen of Rhode Island interested in the early history of his State, every scholar of antiquarian tastes, every Baptist reverencing his ecclesiastical forefathers and wishing to know more of their beliefs, practices, and lives, every Christian, of whatever denomination, to whom American church history seems as important as the church history of former ages—all these, I am sure, will read with great pleasure and profit the "Diary of John Comer," will be glad to find it elucidated by the scholarly and helpful notes which accompany the text, and will be grateful for the publication of the work.

The task of editing and annotating the "Diary of John Comer" was wisely committed, some years ago, by the Rhode Island Historical Society to the Rev. Dr. Barrows, then Pastor of the First Baptist Church, of Newport. He had already made a profound study of the ecclesiastical history of Rhode Island. He had resided for many years at Newport, was familiar with its localities, its history, and its traditions, and was pastor of the ancient church to which John Comer ministered. He brought to his work ample ability, habits of diligent and painstaking research, and a remarkably well-balanced and trained power of historical judgment. He had advanced far toward its completion when his labors were terminated by his unexpected and lamented death.

The manuscript notes and memoranda which he left were placed in my hands to prepare the work for the press. I found the great body of the notes in a state of admirable readiness. It was necessary only to look them over with a view to the correction of clerical errors, and these were very few indeed. Two or three notes I have been able to furnish from the author's memoranda in pencil. In quite a number of cases he had indicated his purpose to make other notes, of which no trace could be found. He had undoubtedly passed them, intending later to supply the deficiency—probably, after farther research. These I have not been able to prepare, being without access to the requisite authorities. My own additions are indicated by my initials.

It is a matter of great regret that the editor was prevented by death from finishing his work, especially because in the final form, which it would have received at his hands, it would, I think, have furnished additional light on some interesting subjects. For example: it is well known that a friendly rivalry exists between the First Baptist Church of Providence and the First Baptist Church at Newport, for the honor of being acknowledged as the oldest existing Baptist church in America. Dr. Barrows, in a very gracious and historical spirit, was an advocate of the claim of the First Church at Newport, having a firm conviction of its validity, and being well aquainted with the facts and authorities on which that claim is based. A note indicated but not written might (I conjecture) have thrown some light upon this question. I am sure that the friends of both churches, and all who are interested in historical researches, will regret that Dr. Barrows was prevented from saying whatever he may have desired to say upon this matter of historical fact. Again, I am almost sure that some fuller notice of the life, work, and character of that great and good man, John Clarke, would have been found in these notes if the author had been permitted to prepare them for the press. It is known that he had under advisement the project of preparing a life of John Clarke; a work which would have been of great value, and for which he had every qualification. Also, it is natural to suppose, that the editor would not have failed to give fuller details of the last days and labors of John Comer than I have been able to supply, and that he would have given some account of his posterity. A son, named also John Comer, was—according to

Morgan Edwards and Backus—a member of the Baptist church in Warren, R. I. This and much more would, I presume, have been traced out and recorded. But God has willed otherwise, and we bow with submission to his will, thankful that the careful and scholarly method of Dr. Barrows enables us to rescue from loss and give to the public such a large and valuable portion of what he had intended to contribute to history. It only remains to give a brief notice of his life and character, and to pay a brief tribute to his memory.

COMFORT EDWIN BARROWS was born in Attleboro, Mass., December 11, 1831; was baptized at Providence, R. I., by S. W. Field, D.D., May 25, 1850, becoming a member of the Central Baptist Church (Old "Pine Street"); was graduated from Brown University in 1858, and from the Theological Institution at Newton in 1861. He was almost immediately settled as pastor of the Baptist church at South Danvers (now Peabody), Mass., where he was ordained December 25, 1861. He removed to Newport, R. I., in 1865, settling as pastor with the First Baptist Church, and remaining in that relation almost nineteen years and until his death, which occurred, after a brief illness, December 26, 1883.

He gave his whole heart to his work. He was a faithful pastor, an instructive and thoroughly biblical preacher, a wise administrator, and a diligent student. He made large acquirements in biblical and theological learning. He had a special fondness for the study of philosophy, Christian doctrine, and church history. His personal character was marked by spotless integrity and purity, deep and spiritual piety, and manly firmness, and was adorned by courtesy, sympathy, and gentleness.

Such a man's work could not be circumscribed by "parish limits." He was known in Newport not only as a chief factor in the religious life of the town, but also as a respected and influential citizen, interested in all benevolent and literary projects. He rose to a high position in his denomination. He not only wrote an able and valuable historical sketch of "The Development of Baptist Principles in Rhode Island"[1]—as well as other small works—but in many ways he helped to *make* history. He had positive convictions concerning Christian doctrine and church order, based upon his study of the Bible—the one authority which he reverently accepted as final and infallible. These convictions made him a regular Baptist of the American type, and circumstances made him a special champion of certain essential features of Baptist doctrine

---

[1] One of the publications of the American Baptist Publication Society.

and practice. By no means disposed to contention, or even to controversy, with a mind of judicial temper, he never shrank from the path of duty. He knew how to promote and defend what he believed to be the cause of truth and of Christ himself, with patient persistence and with vigilance, firmness, and wisdom. He knew also how to act this important part without rashness or bitterness in a broad and moderate spirit, without compromise and yet with abounding charity to all, "speaking the truth in love." He was, therefore, by the grace of God, equal to every emergency, and his influence continually grew. The fruits of his labors and of his leadership remain his noblest monument.

He was frequently called to positions of honor and trust. He was twice chosen President of the Rhode Island Baptist State Convention; was elected trustee of Brown University in 1878, and was, for one term at least, on the Board of Managers of the American Baptist Missionary Union. He received the honorary degree of Doctor in Divinity from Colby University, in 1881.

It will surprise no one who reads his notes in this volume, to know that in the necrology of his *alma mater* it is said of him that "he had a true historic spirit, which became stronger and more active by investigations and writings, which were characterized by thoroughness and accuracy, by candor and a singleness of devotion to the pursuit and attainment of truth."

The worth of Dr. Barrows was fully known, however, only in the daily walks of pastoral duty and in the sacred enclosure of his home. He was married January 1, 1862. His wife was Harriet Willmarth, the eldest daughter of the Rev. Erastus Willard, for more than twenty years Baptist missionary in France. Mrs. Barrows was a woman of high mental and social endowments, and "the heart of her husband safely trusted in her."

Her death, March 13, 1883, was a crushing blow to him, and at first it seemed that he would never rally from it. At length, however, he had risen above the first stunning shock of his great affliction, and had girded himself to return to "life and to duty with undismayed heart." The touching dedication of this volume to the memory of the departed wife, shows at once the depth of his undying affection and his brave resolve, inspired by her memory, to devote himself to "higher service" for God and for mankind. This dedication I regard as a precious souvenir of them both. I found it, in pencil, among the notes and memoranda, and it is given *verbatim* as its author left it. Its last words seem almost prophetic. The providence of God has removed him from all earthly endeavor, and his aspiration for "higher service" in this life must remain unfulfilled; but all who knew him and loved him will take comfort in the assurance that he has only been called to a *higher service*, indeed, in a more perfect life.

The *Comer* of the olden time, with his simple faith and quaint ways, the *Barrows* of the later time, with his riper culture and wider knowledge, but with equal faith in God and in his Holy Word—both faithful workmen in the same vineyard; both true servants of the same Master; both worthy successors of John Clarke; both having hearts loyal to God and sturdy in obedience to him and the defense of his truth; both loving and lovable in the daily walks of life; both called to "higher service" in the midst of their usefulness and promise—in this volume clasp hands across the generations, and being dead, yet speak.

JAMES W. WILLMARTH.

ROXBOROUGH, PHILADELPHIA, Oct. 15, 1892.

Remember the former things of old, for I am God and there is none else.—Isa. 46 : 9.

And thou shalt remember all the way which Jehovah thy God has led thee.—Deut. 8 : 2.

So, on and on, through many an opening door,
 That gladly opens to the key I bring,
 From brightening court to court of Christ, my King,
Hope-fed, love-fed, I journey evermore.

At last I trust these changing scenes will cease;
 There is a court I hear where he abides;
 No door beyond that further glory hides:
My host at home, all change is changed to peace.
WILLIAM C. WILKINSON.

THE DIARY OF
John Comer

Aug. 1, 1704. I BEGIN this book in ye first place with an account of my birth which was on ye first day of August in ye year, on Tuesday, 1704.

The place of my nativity was Boston in N. England. I was the eldest son of my parents, viz. Mr. John and Mrs. Mary Comer.

I desire to eye ye singular Providence of God in granting my birth in a land of gospel light where I was favoured with a religious education, having each of my grandmothers, viz. Mrs. Elinor Comer and Mrs. Mary Pittom, noted among ye godly for eminent and exemplary piety.

July 12, 1706. My dear and honoured father, Mr. John Comer, engaged in a voyage to England, but touching first at South Carolina was soon taken sick with ye prevailing sickness of yt country, and in a few days exchanged as I trust *Earth* for *Heaven*, on ye 12th of July 1706, in ye 32d year of his age, I then lacking about 3 weeks of two years of age.

'Tis notable yt the very night he died he appeared to my mother, being then in Boston, with a bloody handkerchief in his hand. Note, he bled much in his sickness.

1708. This spring I was put to school to Mrs. Gibson, and continued wth her some years, till I came to remember some things myself. I bless God for ye care taken of me when I was so young yt I might learn to read ye holy Scriptures.

July 1. This day my mother was married to Mr. John Phillips, of Boston, by whom she had two children, a son and a daughter.

Aug. 1, 1709. This day I was five years old. This year I first remembered things; the first thing was my dear grandmother Mrs. Mary Pittom taking me into her chamber every evening before I went to bed, and she kneeling down by ye bedside caused me to do so too and used to dedicate me to ye Lord. I to this day (and hope ever shall) remember that one sentence in her prayer, viz. Lord remember this child and make it thine in ye day when thou makest up thy jewels for Christ's sake.

My mother has told me y^t this year I read my Bible half out.

This year my father's mother died; this grandmother was a very eminent woman for exemplary piety.

The holy do they live here forever?

March, 1711. This month my mother's mother died suddenly. She got up well in ye morning and died about noon. Blessed are ye dead y^t die in ye Lord. She was taken speechless at ye first stroke.

This year I was put to school to Mr. Ames Angier,[1] in Boston.

October. I think this month was ye great fire in Boston in a very dreadful manner,[2] about 100 houses burnt, together with ye old meeting house and town house. A drunken woman living near ye meeting house carelessly set some oacom [oakum] on fire, and so fir'd her house, etc.

Blessed be ye Lord for his remembering mercy at y^t time, My mother was y^n burnt out and had like to have lost her life. I was sick at y^t time at my aunt's.

---

[1] Ames Angier (or Anger, as the name is sometimes spelled) was born in Rehoboth, January 29, 1681. His father was the Rev. Samuel Angier, minister in Rehoboth, and his mother was the only child of the Rev. Urian Oakes, fourth president of Harvard College. His name, Ames, came from his paternal grandmother, who was the daughter of the famous William Ames. He was graduated from Harvard College in 1701, and in 1708 was married to Margaret McCarty. The winter before his graduation he taught school in Charlestown, the contract bearing date November 21, 1700, receiving as compensation £30 in money, and a small quantity of wood. He became the first master of the school established about 1717 at the corner of West and Common (now Tremont) Sts, Boston. Early in the year 1720, he "was chosen schoolmaster for a writing school at the south part of the town at 100 pounds per annum." He died in the latter part of the year 1720.

For these items, as well as for other facts embodied in the following notes, the editor is indebted to the kindness of John L. Sibley, M. A., Librarian Emeritus of Harvard College, whose two ample volumes of 1175 pages on "Harvard Graduates" are a noble contribution to the history of his Alma Mater. The second volume reaches down only to 1677.

[2] "The fire of 1711, the most sweeping and disastrous that had yet occurred, burned down all the houses, some of them very capacious buildings, on both sides of Cornhill from School Street to Dock Square, besides the First Church, the Town House, all the upper part of King's Street, and the greater part of Pudding Lane. In all, nearly one hundred houses were destroyed, of which the rubbish taken from the ruins was used to fill up Long wharf. 'Thus the town of Boston,' says the Rev. Cotton Mather, in his sermon on the event, 'just going to get beyond fourscore years of age, and conflicting with much labor and sorrow, is, a very vital and valuable part of it, soon cut off and flown away.'"— *Memorial Hist. Bost.*, *II.*, 504.

Aug., 1713.   In this year (I think) as I was playing a childish play on a tilter [a teeter] with one *Power Merit*, one of my schoolmates, near a cellar, I fell, by reason of a sudden jerk, off into it, among some stones, and cut my head and tongue so y^t it hung out of my mouth unless kept in by a muffler, and none thought I should ever be able to speak plain again; for by ye fall I was entirely senseless. But in about 4 months by a constant supply of honey in my [mouth] it was healed; and y^t God who is a God working wonders gave me ye free use of y^t member again, beyond all expectation.

1714.   This summer my mother with my father-in-law [stepfather] went over to South Carolina to live. One principal reason was because he had got two hundred pounds in money from my mother y^t my own father left for my education, and upon my grandfather's hearing of it he pursued him to get it; but he went away thither privately. So I was abused. But God has promised to avenge ye wrongs of ye fatherless. He lived there about two years and at ye expiration of y^m, he having been out on his horse came home in a dark evening and going into the house came out to look after his horse with a long pipe in his mouth, it being very dark fell over a log, ye pipe stem ran down his throat and broke and all means y^t could be used could not get it out. It being Saturday, he continued till Monday without speaking and died. Thus ye Lord found out a way in his Providence (tho awful) to meet with him. I always thought it a judgment.

1715.   This year took some notice of God's goodness to me, and began to see so much as excited me to look to God in a way of prayer, being I hope in some measure made sensible of my sinfulness and unworthiness and of the need I had of Divine preservation. To the best of my remembrance the Providence y^t first stir'd me up was the surprising death of a little lad about my age, his name was William Thomas, who was playing marvils [marbles] near the Old North Meeting House, Boston, and a cart laden passing by, a marvil rolling under the cart he stept to get it, the horse starting run ye wheel over his head and brake it so y^t his brains came out and he died on y^e . . . He was carried into Mr. Sunderlain's house, where I saw him together with multitudes of others; he look'd awfully. O how my soul seemed at y^t time when mine eye affected my heart wonderfully. I thought, were it my case to lie so bruised and broken, and to have my soul fly into the world of spirits, how would it be? I was lost in myself. But this I knew, I was strong [ly] affected wth it. The next Lord's Day, Dr. Cotton Mather,³ I remember well, preached from these suitable words: In ye morning it flourisheth and groweth up, but in ye evening 'tis cut down and withereth. This first awakened me.

Aug. 1, 1716.   This day I was twelve years old. I remember 'tis remarked of my dear Redeemer y^t at this age he was found disputing in ye midst of ye Doctors both hearing and asking y^m questions. Luk. 2 : 42, 46. O may I conform to Christ in all things possible; may I be willing to hear and ask about good things.

'Tis remark'd y^t Saint Ignatius was of this age at Christ's crucifixion, and y^t he was the child y^t he took up in his arms to teach his disciples humility. O may I be humble; I am sure a sense of my sinfulness is enough to make me so. May I be so in deed and in truth.

March, 1718.   I having been disappointed by my father-in-law [stepfather], by his taking my money from me, of a liberal education, ye time being near y^t I must be put out to learn a trade, and this month there was great concern about one, my grandfather inclined to a tailor's trade, but my [mind] was bent upon studying. Only at length 'twas concluded y^t I should learn a glover's trade, and Mr. Benjamin Harris was pitch't upon. After many intreaties I was prevailed upon to comply, and, since it must be so, I chose him because my own cousin Thomas Dolbear was just gone to the same place being of my age.

May.   This month I went to learn ye glover's trade of Mr. Benjamin Harris, of Boston.

Aug. 1.   This day I am fourteen years of age. This day I was bound⁴ by my Grandfather, Mr. Jno. Comer, for

---

³ Cotton Mather, son of the Rev. Increase Mather and Maria, daughter of the Rev. John Cotton, was born in Boston, February 12, 1662-63. He entered Harvard College at the age of twelve, and was graduated in the year 1678, and May 13, 1685, was ordained colleague with his father, over the North Church [Congregational] in Boston, which position he held till his death, February 13, 1728. In 1710, he received from the University of Glasgow the honorary degree of Doctor of Divinity, being the first American thus honored by a British university. "His learning was probably more varied and extensive than that of any other person in America."—Sprague, *Annals of the Amer. Pulpit.*

⁴ The laws relating to the trades were early transferred from the Old to the New World, so far as the nature of the case would permit. In the several Colonies, the statutes relating to the service of minors were borrowed from English legislation. Early in the reign of Elizabeth, "it was enacted that no person should exercise a trade or mystery without having served a seven years' apprenticeship." "This period was thought no more than sufficient to instruct the learner in his profession, craft, or mystery, under a properly

7 years, to Mr. Benjamin Harris. Eph. 6 : 5, 6, 7 ; 1 Cor. 7 : 22.

This day I am fifteen years old.

Aug. 1, 1719. I continued in my apprenticeship. I had opportunity to read and did improve it; for Mr. Harris gave himself to drinking and company-keeping to excess, and minded nothing of his business. Myself and my cousin fared very hardly, and on all accounts things went ill as to us in the family; tho I hope God blessed the time to me.

This year I composed a set discourse (w^h was ye first) from y^t word, Ecc. 12 : 1: Remember now . . . May I do so.

I find elevated thought in myself a sin y^t those of my age I plainly see are addicted to. Young company entices to merriment. Lord help me to watch against all appearance of evil, and help me to perform all things that are good.

O unhappy family y^t I am cast into. No show of good; neither power nor form of godliness. Only lifeless prayer on the evening of the Sabbath; and drink with gaming all ye week.

June, 1720. This month my mother took me from Mr. Harris' service because of the extremity of the circumstances of his family. Tho he made many words, he saw he could do nothing, because my Indenture was not authentick—made without my Mother's knowledge or consent, only by my Grandfather.

I liv'd with him 2 years and one month. Yet 'twas thought advisable y^t I should follow ye same trade (which I always abhor'd).

July. This month I was put by my Grandfather to Mr. Zechariah Fitch, of Boston, of ye same trade. He observing me to read much, frequently said to me and to others, I see you won't do for me, for you read *too much*. At this time I applied myself to my Grandfather to go on in studying, but he refused. I prevailed upon ye Rev^d. Dr. Increase Mather[5] to go and ask him, which being done he consented to it.

---

qualified master, teacher, or doctor—for these terms were synonymous—and to reimburse the latter by service for the training received." The origin of the custom of apprenticeship is involved in some obscurity. "So far as can be seen it arose in the Middle Ages." "The formation of guilds and corporations of tradesmen in England dates probably from the twelfth century, and it is almost certain that the institution of apprenticeships cannot be of much later date."—*Ency. Brittan.* Not till within the present century did compulsory give place to voluntary apprenticeship. Reforms of abuses incident to the system were among the noble achievements of Adam Smith.

[5] Increase Mather, son of Richard Mather and Catharine Hoult, was born at Dorchester, June 21, 1639. At the age of twelve, he entered Harvard College, and was graduated in the class of 1656. In July of the following year he sailed for England in response to an

December. This month I began my grammar with my old schoolmaster, Mr. Ames Angier, being 16 years and four months old. Thus I set out upon my studies.

April, 1721. The latter end of this month the small pox [6] was brought into Boston, which was exceeding surprising to me. The first man who brought it in died.

The distemper prevailing in town, some of ye youth of my acquaintance were taken away by death, which by God's blessing tended to blow up ye coal of conviction in my soul and to keep it alive. I thought much about ye angel slaying in ye camp of ye Assyrians, as ye sickness prevailed. This put me on ye duty of self-examination and crying to ye Lord for ye magnifying his grace towards me.

Aug. 1. Being this day seventeen years old, I set it apart as a day of solemn fasting and supplication in my chamber, to humble my soul before the Lord; to bewail the sins of my youth and of my nature which is ye woful spring of all actual transgressions. I bemoaned myself before the Lord in secret, and between each prayer I spent ye time in close examination and in reading Mr. Vincent's [7] book, entitled *Christ's certain*

---

invitation from his brother Samuel, who was then a minister in Dublin, Ireland. He enrolled himself as a student in Trinity College, and when but nineteen years of age received the Master's degree. Returning home, he married, March 6, 1662, Maria, daughter of the celebrated Rev. John Cotton, and, May 27, 1664, became pastor of the North Church in Boston, and continued in that office till his death, meanwhile serving as President of Harvard College from 1684 till 1701. The corporation and overseers of the College presented him in 16.'2 with a diploma of Doctor of Divinity, this being "the first instance in which such a degree was conferred in British America." He died August 23, 1723, aged 84 years.—Sprague's *Annals*.

[6] The fear expressed by Mr. Comer in his diary, was characteristic of the age. The small pox was at that time, doubtless, the most dreaded of all the scourges that afflict mankind. "Having been twenty years in abeyance, it renewed its dreaded visitation in 1721. Nearly six thousand persons took it in Boston, of whom nearly one thousand died in the year."—*Memor. Hist. Bost.*, II., 52. During the time of its prevalence, it received the earnest attention of medical men, who sought to compel it to yield to their treatment. And the studies thus bestowed were crowned with a good degree of success. A wonderful discovery was made, and the practice of inoculation was introduced.

We have a curious glimpse of the prevalence of the small pox, and of the dread with which it was regarded, in a letter written by the Rev. Joseph Bellamy, January 23, 1754. Called from his rural parish in Connecticut, to become pastor of the Presbyterian church in New York city, he laid the case, after having informally declined once and again, before the Convocation of Litchfield County for final decision, earnestly hoping they would counsel him not to go, citing to them among other reasons for not going this, "I may die with the small pox, and leave a widow and fatherless children in a helpless condition."

[7] This was Thomas Vincent, a man of considerable influence in his day; was educated at Oxford; became minister of St. Mary Magdalene Church in London; was one of the ministers ejected in 1662 for Nonconformity; subsequently, preached at Noxton until his death in 1678. During the plague in London, in 1665, he was distinguished for his constant and

and sudden appearance to judgment; which I hope was made of some use to me. In ye close of ye day I resolved by the help of Christ, that if the Lord saw meet to visit me with the small pox (which I no way expected to escape) and would raise me up again, I would study the advancement of his glory; and walk in the observation of all gospel duties, even to the commemoration of his dying love at his holy table. After ye going down of ye sun I visited my Grandfather, who was then sick and laboured under ye infirmities of old age; whom it pleased God to call hence as I trust into ye joy of his Lord, on Monday, Augt ye 7th, 1721.

He committed me to the care and inspection of ye Rev^d. Mr. Jno Weeb [Webb][8] and by will bequeathed to me £500. I would eye this favor and esteem it as coming from God. This sum was to bring me up and introduce me comfortably in ye world, which it did. Tho there is *one* would have had it otherwise, but God's holy Providence provided, and diverted all contrary advices. I may comfortably take up that word Hos. 14 : 3; Jer. 49 : 11.

Finding w^t comfortable provision God had made for me, I acquainted Mr. Weeb [Webb] of my extreme fear of ye small pox, upon which he advised me to go to school out of town. Thereupon, on ye 15th of Aug^t, I left my former master Mr. Angier and went and boarded at Mr. Ephraim Ezbone's [Osborn's], about a mile and ½ from Cambridge, and was recommended to Mr. Saml Danforth,[9] schoolmaster of Cambridge. After I was ad-

---

disinterested activity in behalf of the sufferers. He was the author of several works, most of them passing through many editions. A catalogue of them is given in Wood's *Athen. Oxon.* III., 117 l. He had at one time a controversy with William Penn. Edmund Callamy says in his *Ejected Ministers*, II., 32, that he " was a worthy, humble, and eminently pious man, of sober principles, and great zeal and diligence."

The above work on *Christ's Certain and Sudden Appearance to Judgment* was first published in 1667 as an 8vo; was published again in 1669 as a 12mo; the sixth edition appeared in 1683; the tenth edition in Glasgow in 1723. It has been once republished in this country, at Greenfield, Mass., in 1816, a copy of which is in the library of Harvard College.—Allibone's *Dict. of Authors.*

[8] "John Webb was born at Braintree, Mass., was graduated at Harvard College in 1708; was ordained first pastor of the New North Church, Boston, October 20, 1714; received the Rev. Peter Thatcher as colleague in 1720; after Mr. Thatcher's death in 1738 was sole pastor until 1742, when the Rev. Andrew Eliot was ordained as his colleague; and died April 16, 1750."—Sprague's *Annals.*

[9] Samuel Danforth, son of the Rev. John Danforth (H. C. 1677), of Dorchester, Mass., and a grandson of the Rev. Samuel Danforth (H. C. 1643), of Roxbury, Mass., was graduated from Harvard College in 1715; was schoolmaster in Cambridge in 1724, and had been for some time previously; married, August 14, 1726, Elizabeth Symmes; died October 27, 1777, aged about eighty-one years. He early left the vocation of schoolmaster; held several civil and judicial offices; was Judge of Probate and also of Common Pleas. During the Revolution he was a royalist.—Lucius R. Paige, *Hist. of Cambridge, Mass.*

mitted into yᵉ school, and settled in a religious family, I thought myself exceeding happy and hoped I should not be visited wᵗʰ yᵉ prevailing distemper yᵗ was raging in Boston, which I so much feared. My hopes upon yᵗ account were soon disappointed and cut off; for yᵉ Lord by a strange and undiscovered way and means sent it into yᵉ very family *and no other* in yᵉ neighborhood; yᵉ

October. beginning, Mr. Ozbon's [Osborn's] youngest daughter was visited with it, and in 10 days she died. Tis beyond expression to relate wᵗ trouble I was then filled withal at yᵗ amazing instant. But upon its breaking out here I betook myself to the house of Mr. Jonathan Steadman, in yᵉ middle of yᵉ town of Cambridge, so yᵗ notwithstanding my extreme trouble, I kept to school. Nevertheless scruples arose mightily in me at yᵗ time whether my remove from Boston was not sinful, all things considered, and highly displeasing to God; for I going from Boston to escape it, and yᵗ coming only into yᵉ family I was in, I thought it look't like Jonah's flying from the presence of the Lord; wʰ word was a very great aggravation of my trouble. On or about

Oct. 30, having taken a solitary walk as far as yᵉ Royal Oak, which is about a mile out of town towards Charlestown, being in a praying posture with my hat in my hand, near the 3 mile stone, I used such uncommon expressions as these, being in deep distress of soul: Lord, If it be thy holy will yᵗ I should be visited wᵗʰ yᵉ small pox, I pray thee yᵗ if I am for life and there is still any work for me to do for the people yᵗ I may have my fears continued concerning my death till yᵉ instant yᵗ I know yᵉ small pox is broke out upon me; and then as a token yᵗ I shall live to show forth thy praises let my mind be composed under the visitation; let this be a token to me of my life for thy goodness' sake, O Lord. After this I was exceedingly grieved fearing it was an unlawful petition and yᵗ yᵉ glorious God would be offended at it rather yⁿ answer it.

About this time yᵉ practice of Innoculation [10] was set up and

---

[10] Inoculation as a preventative of small pox did not become generally known in England till after the year 1717, when Lady Montague wrote her celebrated letter from Adrianople. And not till more than a quarter of a century after its introduction did it become firmly established. It encountered bitter opposition from the learned, and especially from the medical profession. Moore, in his *History of Small-pox*, written in 1815, states that at the beginning of the eighteenth century about one-fourteenth of the population died of small pox, while at the close of the century the number had increased to one-tenth. The friends of the new practice in England received, however, instruction and encouragement from across the water. In 1722, Mr. Neal gave to the public "A Narrative of the method

much esteemed of. Doctor Zabdial Boylstone[11] was y̆e chief actor in it. The College and School broke up. Mr. Nicholas Cever [Sever][12] one of y̆e fellows and Mr. Sam¹ Danforth y̆e schoolmaster passed under y̆e operation. Upon this I joined wth the lawfulness of y̆e practice of Innoculation (tho some wrote and printed against it), and concluded to pass under it. Accordingly, I repaired home to Boston on

Nov. 4. Being Saturday and rainy weather I thought to omit it till Monday; and on y̆e Lord's Day y̆e

5. I went to meeting at New North meeting and being there, a young man just recovered who smelt exceedingly strong gave it me, or I catch't it of him; it overpowered me so y̆t I was disordered all sermon time. Returning home I informed of y̆t affair, and expected it working in a fortnight. So I was prevented from Innoculation. As to y̆e soul amazing terror I was in about this time concerning Eternity, 'tis inexpressible.

---

and success of inoculating the small pox in New England, by Mr. Benjamin Colman; with a reply to the objections made against it from principles of conscience, in a letter from a minister at Boston. To which is now prefixed an historical introduction."

[11] Zabdial Boylston, justly distinguished for his persistent and successful efforts to introduce inoculation into this country, was born in Brookline, Mass., 1680; Savage, in his Geneal. Dict., says March 9, 1679. During the prevalence of the small pox in Boston in 1721, which was carrying death into hundreds of homes and casting a deep g'oom over the entire community, he became deeply interested in studying a method of mitigating the violence of the fatal disease. The method proposed was by inoculation. In his progress he was obliged to meet and overcome both ignorance and superstition. He was opposed with warmth and even bitterness on the ground both of science and of religion. Learned physicians spoke and wrote against him. Appeal was made to the conscience to witness against him and his new method. He was even made the object of persecution by the civil authorities. It is reported that his life was threatened. Undismayed by his opponents Dr. Boylston tried the experiment upon his own son, thirteen years of age, and upon two servants in his family, in each case with entire success. During the years 1721-22, he inoculated two hundred and forty-seven persons, and thirty-nine were treated by other physicians; and "of these two hundred and eighty-six cases only six died." By invitation he visited London, where in 1726 he published a book which he dedicated to the Princess Caroline, and was made a Fellow of the Royal Society, "the first American, we believe, ever admitted to that honor." He died March 1, 1766, and was buried in Brookline.— Thacher's *Amer. Med. Biog.*

[12] Nicolas Sever, a fellow and tutor in Harvard College from 1716 to 1728, was born in Roxbury, April 15, 1680, and graduated from Harvard in 1701, one of his classmates being Timothy Cutler, third Rector of Yale College. He preached for a time in Haverhill, and April 11, 1711, was ordained minister in Dover, N. H. He left after a four years' service to become tutor in his *Alma Mater.* He was one of the leaders in a long and bitter controversy in the government of the college, growing out of the liberal spirit shown by Mr. Hollis in connection with his munificent gifts. It was a controversy that became so serious as to threaten "the dissolution of the college." Mr. Sever died April 7, 1764.—Quincey, *Hist. Harv. Univ.* Pierce, *Ibid.*

Nothing but ye gashly [ghastly] countenance of death unprepared for was before me, and no light of a reconciled God, nor a sense of the application of ye sin-cleansing blood of Christ to my distressed soul. I remained in extreme terror until the 22 of Novr. All ye interval of time I spent in looking over ye affairs of my soul and on y^t day I was taken sick. As soon as 'twas told me y^t ye distemper appeared, all my fears entirely vanished away and a beam of comfort darted into my soul and with it a satisfaction from y^t word *thou shalt not die but live and declare the works of the Lord*. Yea, so great was my satisfaction y^t I immediately replied to my Aunt who informed me, Then I know y^t I shall not die now; but gave no reason why I said so. Then the prayer-hearing God was graciously pleased to answer my requests while at Cambridge. So y^t under ye situation when I was in my senses (for I was deprived 4 days) I was supported by y^t good word Ps. 50 : 15. The visitation tho heavy was made light and easy (I was not totally blind) because God's rod and staff comforted me. I lay under it from Nov. 22, to Decemr. 10, on which day I was so far released as to walk abroad.

1722. Being restored to my former health and strength again, after so awful and remarkable a visitation, in which there were between eight and nine hundred snatch'd away by the stroke of death, I resolved to study God's glory as my chief end; and also to follow my studies with my former schoolmaster, Mr. Saml Danforth, of Cambridge, because I delighted in y^t place.

Accordingly I returned to Cambridge in the month of March, at which time ye small pox was spreading there. Among those who died of it (which were about 9), Mr. Saml Steadman, a young gentleman, a physician, was one to whose funeral I was invited and chosen to be a bearer, with w^h I complied. He was a near friend of mine and much in my affection. O cruel death, and yet kind.

July. On ye Commencement Day, one —— Lamb, a student at ye College in an airy fit got out of ye window to go to another chamber, it being ye 3^d story, fell down and received his death wound; so y^t he expired in a few days. May I take warning.

At this school I passed thro many of the Latin authors. Here I took the sweetest satisfaction. Everything about me was pleasant and desirable.

This month in Boston the authorities made parchment money,[13] *i. e.*, a penny, two pence, and 3 pence.

Aug. 1. This day I am eighteen years old. I find myself ensnared with youthful vanities; O how pleasant are they to nature. Lord, grant y^t I may not be drawn from thee. My companions were at this time very near and dear to me, more especially Thomas Prentice, Thomas Graves, John Hovey, and Willm Hobby. Like David and Jonathan to me.

January, 1723. Having ever since my recovery of ye small pox look't upon myself obliged to serve God in a more eminent manner y^n heretofore, and looking on myself as having ye vows of God lying on me to serve him in ye ways of his Holy Institutions and more especially in ye commemoration of his dying love at his table.

Accordingly I earnestly entreated the Lord y^t I might have all ye antecedent qualifications and all actual preparation for it. That word was made useful to me, 1 Cor. 11 : 24, This do in remembrance of me.

Hereupon I resolved to go and present myself to ye Pastor of ye church of Cambridge, Mr. Nathl Appleton,[14] who was willing to encourage my motion to good.

---

[13] Paper currency was first introduced into New England in 1690, and was made necessary by an unsuccessful expedition against Canada under Sir William Phipps. The government had made no provision for paying the soldiers, relying for the purpose upon the booty that should be taken from the enemy. Since there was no money in the treasury, and no time to raise money by a levy upon the country, " resort was made to Paper Money, then called Bills of Credit." Holders of these Bills eventually lost much by their depreciation.

" It is perhaps not generally known," says Mr. Drake, in *Old Landmarks of Boston*, " that a paper currency of small denomination was issued in the Colony (Massachusetts) as early as 1722. They were printed on parchment. No other instance is remembered of the emission of such small sums in paper until we come down to the period of the Revolution. The whole amount authorized was only five hundred pounds, and specimens are very rare." Fac similes are given in the work referred to above. Besides the above-mentioned book, see Drake's *Hist. Bost.*, and Felt's *Hist. Amer. Currency*; also Arnold's *Hist. R. I.*, Vol. II., 39. The latter says that to meet extraordinary expenses incurred in 1710, " Rhode Island adopted the plan pursued by her neighbors. An act for issuing bills of credit was passed. Five thousand pounds in denominations from five pound to two shilling bills were issued, signed the sixteenth of August."

[14] Nathaniel Appleton, for sixty-six years pastor of the church in Cambridge, was a son, of the Hon. John Appleton, one of the king's council, and Elizabeth, daughter of the Rev. John Rogers, fifth President of Harvard College, and was born in Ipswich, December 9, 1693, and graduated from Harvard in 1712, " when he was a little less than nineteen." He was invited, upon the death of the Rev. William Brattle, to become pastor of the Cambridge Church, and received ordination October 9, 1717, Increase Mather preaching the sermon. The same year, 1717, he was elected a Fellow of the college, continuing an honored and useful member of its government till 1779. " In 1771, he received from his *Alma Mater* the

C

Feb. 17. This day I was received into full communion with ye church in Cambridge.

Lord's D., 24. This day was sacrament day; I enjoyed great comfort and satisfaction in attending y^t Sacred Institution of my dear Lord.

On the 24th of Feb. was ye most remarkable tide y^t ever was known in N. England, ye sea rose several feet higher y^n usual. Sunday meetings in Boston broke up on y^t account by people being called to secure things from ye wash of ye sea.

About this time my near companion Mr. Ephraim Craft,[15] who was a member of Mr. Webb's Communion, in Boston, embraced the principle of Believer's Baptism, in opposition to Infant Baptism, and was baptized by Mr. E. Callender,[16] in Boston. In some little time after I met him and manifested my concern about y^t affair (at this time I never in ye least degree doubted ye validity of Infant Baptism); and after some contrary discourse, he earnestly desired me to read Mr. Jos. Stennett's[17] treatise on Baptism, which I consented to, after much

---

degree of Doctor of Divinity, an honor which had been previously conferred by that college upon only one individual, namely, Increase Mather, about eighty years before." He died February 9, 1784.—Elliot, *Biog. Dict.*; Sprague's *Annals*.

[This "church in Cambridge" was, of course, Congregational. Congregational churches of "the standing order," *i. e.*, established by law in Massachusetts and Connecticut, were the leading churches of those colonies; the Baptists then were a small, despised, and persecuted people. In Comer's Diary and the Notes, Congregational churches are often mentioned as "the First," "the North," etc., without denominational designation, as was the current custom in John Comer's time, for the obvious reason just stated. A little attention will show the reader what church is meant in each such case, as distinguished from the Baptist churches often spoken of. We note, in passing, that John Comer, at first a Congregationalist, though a sturdy Baptist, without thought of compromise, and unflinchingly true to his convictions, cultivated friendships with good men of other denominations, including those of the communion he had left. For example, he evidently esteemed Rev. Mr Clap, Congregational pastor at Newport, and often visited him.—J. W. W.]

[15] Ephraim Craft was baptized into the First Baptist Church in Boston, January 12, 1723.

[16] Elisha Callender, for twenty years (1718–1738) pastor of the First Baptist Church in Boston, was a son of the Rev. Ellis Callender, born in Boston in 1680 and graduated from Harvard College in 1710. He was the first Baptist minister in the country who received his collegiate education in the New World. He was baptized August 10, 1713, and five years later, May 21, 1718, was ordained pastor of the church to which his father had long ministered. At this ordination service, when Dr. Increase Mather preached the sermon, there were at least two persons present who remembered the nailing up of the meeting house doors by order of government, namely, Rev. Ellis Callender and Deacon Benjamin Sweetzer. Mr. Callender was a cultivated man. A correspondence which he maintained with friends in London was productive of rich pecuniary blessing to his *Alma Mater*. Mr. Thomas Hollis became a munificent benefactor of Harvard College. Mr. Callender's death occurred very suddenly, in the midst of his usefulness, March 31, 1738.—Cathcart, *Bap. Ency.*; Sprague's *Ann.*

[17] Joseph Stennett, son of Edward Stennett, a minister of some distinction during the

persuasion; he lent it to me (I did not do it with ye view to gain light but only to make objection, hoping to find many flaws in it) and I resolved to turn to every Scripture quoted, and not to take any one without, and in my so doing I found I had never duly considered ye 8 of ye Acts, ye 3 of Matt, and ye 6th of Romans, and such like places.

Hereupon I got (tho privately) books on ye other side ye controversie and found y^m if weighed in ye balance wanting.

After serious and mature deliberation and earnest prayer to ye Lord, I found ye churches not so fully in order in ye point of Baptism as they should be, tho I valued y^m as ye Spouse of Christ and would willingly maintain my communion with y^m.

But to take up such a cross in my early days, when I had not one relative in ye world of y^t mind, was exceeding difficult, so y^t I feared to let my mind in this case be known to any one soul, and being newly admitted into full communion with ye church in Cambridge, I feared it would be hurtful to ye churches and displeasing to God.

So tho I was satisfied y^t my Baptism was defective, I still kept in the communion of ye church (being Congregational and in y^t right as well as in ye essentials of religion); I deviated in my mind in no one point save y^t, viz. ye mode and subject of Baptism.

I communed with several churches in ye same order as I had opportunity in ye course of Divine Providence. The Old North in Boston,[18] Mr. Cotton Mather, Pastor; the New North in Bos-

---

Parliamentary war, was born in Berks County, England, in 1663, and ordained March 4, 1690, pastor of the Sabbatarian church, meeting in Pinner's Hall, London, in which office he remained till his death, which occurred July 11, 1713. On Sundays he ministered to other Baptist churches He was a fine Hebrew scholar, and "composed many beautiful hymns which are still used in the church." In 1702, he published "an admirable defense of baptism," in reply to Mr. David Russen's book, entitled "Fundamentals without a Foundation." This "Defense" is doubtless the treatise to which Mr. Comer refers. —Irving, *Hist. Eng. Baptists*, II., 481-502; Cathcart, *Bap. Ency.*

[18] There were in Boston previous to 1730, seven Congregational churches: First Church (1630), known as the Old Church; Second Church (1650), known as the North Church, then as the Old North; Third Church (1669), known as the South Church, then as the Old South; Brattle Street Church (1699); New North Church (1714); New South Church (1719), and Federal Street Church (1727).

Besides these there were a few of other names. Mr. Daniel Neal, writing in 1720, says, "There are ten churches or places of public worship in Boston: six of Establishment, namely, the Old Church, so called, because 'tis the mother of all the rest, whereof the Rev. Mr. Wadsworth, and Mr. Thomas Foxcroft are pastors; the North Church, whereof the Doctors Increase and Cotton Mather are pastors; the South Church, whereof the Rev. Mr. Joseph Sewell and Mr Thomas Prince are pastors; the church in Brattle Street, whereof the Rev. Mr. Benjamin Coleman and Mr. William Cooper are pastors. The other two churches are lately built, and are called the New North, and the New South; Mr. John Webb being pastor of

ton,[19] Mr. John Webb, Pastor; the New Brick in Boston,[20] Mr. Will[m] Waldron,[21] Pastor; the church at Andover,[22] Mr. John

the one, and Mr Samuel Chickley of the other. But besides the forementioned churches, which are properly the Establishment of the Country, there is one Episcopal church, one French, one Anabaptist, and one Congregation of Quakers. The Quakers are but few in number, though they are treated at present with as much candour and goodness as they can reasonably desire; the Anabaptists are likewise but few, but serious, modest, humble Christians. Mr. Elisha Callender is their present pastor."—Neal, *Hist. N. Eng.*, II., 227.

The Old North, or Second Church in Boston, was formed in 1650. For twenty years one meeting house had accommodated the whole population of the town. In the year 1648, however, the number of inhabitants had so increased that another was deemed absolutely necessary for their accommodation. It was therefore agreed that one should be built at the North End, the foundation being laid the following year. To distinguish it from the other, this Second Church was called the North, and in time the Old North. It was sometimes designated the "Church of the Mathers," because it was for so many years presided over by different members of this eminent family. Samuel Mather preached here for a short time when it was first formed, though he is not reckoned among its pastors. As given by the Rev. Chandler Robbins, the early pastors of the church were, John Mayo (1655-1672), Increase Mather (1664-1723), Cotton Mather (1685-1728). During the Revolution this church lost its meeting house, when it was united with the New Brick Church, the consolidated body retaining the name and records of the Second Church.—Chandler Robbins, *Hist. North Ch.*; *Mem. Hist. Bost.*

[19] The New North Church was organized in 1714, "seventeen substantial mechanics forming the nucleus" of the body. John Webb was ordained the first pastor. In accordance with the custom of the times the church desired, in 1720, to call an assistant pastor. The choice, which fell on Peter Thatcher, was not unanimous; indeed he had a bare majority of one vote, and that was cast by the pastor, Mr. Webb. A division was created, and a number of members withdrew. Nevertheless, Mr. Thatcher continued to serve the church as assistant pastor until his death. The meeting house was built on the corner of Clark and Hanover, then called North Street.—Ephraim Elliot, *Hist. New North Ch.*

[20] The New Brick Church had its origin in the division in the New North Church occasioned by the calling of the Rev. Peter Thatcher. The organization was effected in 1722. William Waldron was ordained the first pastor. The meeting house, fronting on Hanover Street, was built of brick, the first in the town, and was elegant for the times; it was dedicated May 10, 1721. This house became subsequently the home of the Second Church, by which the New Brick Church was absorbed.—Chandler Robbins, *Hist. New Brick Ch.*

[21] William Waldron, son of Captain Richard Waldron and Elinor Vaughan, was born in Portsmouth, N. H., November 4, 1697, and graduated from Harvard College in 1717. When the New Brick Church in Boston was formed, he was chosen pastor and was ordained May 22, 1722, Cotton Mather preaching the sermon. Soon after his ordination, he married Eliza Allen, by whom he had two children, one of them subsequently becoming the wife of Josiah Quincey, of Braintree, Mass. After having preached but six short years he was taken suddenly sick while on a visit to a friend, the Rev. William Cooper, minister of the Brattle Street Church, and died November 11, 1727.—Sprague's *Annals*.

[22] "The church of Andover was organized October 24, 1645. The first meeting house was built near the old burying ground in North Andover, and stood till 1711. The larger portion of the inhabitants, for several years after settlement, lived in that part of the town. When, however, in 1707, it was thought necessary to build a new meeting house, the votes of the town show that the bulk of the population was in the southerly part. For, 'September 9, 1707, voted to set the meeting house on th' spot of ground near the wood call'd Holt's Wood, where the cross paths meet at the southwest corner of George Abbot's ground.' This was objected to on the ground that it would greatly incommode the Rev. Mr. Barnard, who lived near the old meeting house. A division took place into

Barnard,[23] Pastor; the church at Newport,[24] Mr. Nath[1] Clap,[25] Pastor; the church at New Haven,[26] Mr. Joseph Noice,[27] Pastor.

North and South Parishes, John Barnard remaining with the North. Pastors of South Church, Andover, Samuel Phillips, 1711-1771; Jonathan French, 1772-1809." [*Historical Manual of the South Church, Andover, by George Mowar,* 1859.]
Pastors of First Andover Church, John Woodbridge, 16.4; Francis Dane, 1649-1697; Thomas Barnard, 1682-1718; John Barnard, 1710-1757. Church was divided under Thomas Barnard about location of a meeting house. [*See Abbot's History of Andover.*]

[23] John Barnard, son of the Rev. Thomas (H. C., 1679), was born in Andover, Mass., February 26, 1690, and graduated from Harvard College in 1709. After a few years spent in teaching, he became his father's successor as minister of the North Parish of Andover, being ordained, April 8, 1719. He died while still in office, June 14, 1757. "The people for seventy years," during the ministry of father and son, were greatly prospered.—Sprague's *Annals*.

[24] Though the Rev. Mr. Clap had with great fidelity continued to preach in Newport from 1695, no Congregational church was formed until 1720. Only eight years after this result had been achieved, a second church was formed on account of some differences that had arisen in the body. The Rev. John Adams, who had been chosen to assist Mr. Clap, became pastor of the new church.
The pastors of these churches were: Of the First Church, Nathaniel Clap (1720-1745), William Vinal (1746-1768), Samuel Hopkins (1770-1803), Caleb J. Tenney (1804-1815), Calvin Hitchcock (1815-1820), Samuel Austin (1821-1826), William H. Beecher (1830-1833). Of the Second Church, John Adams (1728-1730), James Searing (1731-1755), Ezra Stiles (1755-1786), William Patten (1786-1833). During the spring of 1833, the two churches came together and formed the United Congregational Church, choosing for pastor, A. H. Dumont.—T. W. Wood, *MS. Hist. of Ch.*

[25] Nathaniel Clap, son of Nathaniel Clap, was born January, 1668, and graduated from Harvard College, 1690. He began his ministry in Newport, 1695, and after many discouragements succeeded in forming a Congregational church in 1720. Of this church he was ordained pastor on the third of November, and continued in that office until his death, October 30, 1745. His pastorate thus covered a period of twenty-five years, and his entire ministry in Newport a half century. He was never married. He was a man of singular gravity of demeanor. Dean Berkeley, who visited Newport in 1728, said of him: "Before I saw Father Clap, I thought the Bishop of Rome had the gravest aspect of any man I ever saw; but really the minister of Newport has the most venerable appearance." And George Whitefield, who landed in Newport in 1740, remarked: "He looked like a good old Puritan, and gave me an idea of what stamp those men were who first settled New England . . . I could but think that I was sitting with one of the patriarchs."—Ross, *Hist. Desc.*, 143; *Biog Cyclop., R. I.*

[26] (Wanting.)

[27] Joseph Noyes, son of the Rev. James Noyes (Harv. 1659), was born in Stonington, Conn., in 1688, and graduated from Yale College in 1709, and from 1710-1715 served as tutor. President Stiles speaks in very laudatory terms of the great services he rendered the college during his tutorship. He with Mr. Fisk, "were the pillar tutors and the glory of the college." At the death of the Rev. James Pierpont, his father-in-law, Mr. Noyes was invited to the pulpit of the First Church in New Haven, and received ordination July 4, 1716. He was greatly recommended by the celebrity of his father, who was pastor at Stonington, and of his grandfather, who was the first teacher of the church in Newbury, Mass. A few months after his ordination the college was removed from Saybrook to New Haven. During his pastorate a long controversy was waged as to which of two parties into which the church was divided—the two parties maintaining separate meetings—was the First Church; the controversy involved also doctrinal differences. Mr. Noyes died June 14, 1761.—Bacon, *Hist. Disc.*, 239.

These with yᵉ church in Cambridge,[28] Mr. Nathˡ Appleton, Pastor, were 7 in number.

'Twas concluded by Mr. Webb yᵗ I should be forwarded if I would go and studie with a private minister in yᵉ country which I consented to; accordingly Mr. Barnard, of Andover, was pitch't upon, to whom I went in

May, and while I was a student at his house I communed wᵗʰ his church, but laboured under inexpressible difficulties in my mind on yᵉ point of Baptism.

Sept. This month one Cornelius Bennett[29] and I finding we should not yᵗ year be presented to Cambridge Colledge for admittance we resolved to go to New Haven Colledge and offer [ourselves] for admittance there, and accordingly was admitted by yᵉ Revᵈ Mr. Samuel Andrew,[30] Pastor of yᵉ church in Milford[31] and Mr. James Pairpoint [Pierpont],[32] tutor of yᵉ college.

---

[28] The First Congregational Church of Cambridge, Mass., was organized February 1, 1636 (O. S.). The pastors were: Thomas Sheppard, ordained 1636, died 1649; Jonathan Mitchell, ordained 1650, died 1667; Urian Oakes, ordained 1671, died 1681; Nathaniel Gookin, ordained 1682, died 1692; William Brattle, ordained 1696, died 1717; Nathaniel Appleton, ordained 1717, died 1784. [*Eight Lectures on the History of the First Church in Cambridge*, by Alexander Mackenzie, 1873.]

[29] (Wanting.)

[30] Samuel Andrew, second rector of Yale College, was the eldest son of Samuel Andrew, of Cambridge, and was born January 29, 1656; was graduated from Harvard College in 1675. He was ordained minister at Milford, Conn., November 18, 1685. He married Abigail, daughter of Gov. Robert Treat "He was one of the original projectors, founders, and trustees of Yale College; and after the death of Mr. Pierson, the first rector of the college, he was appointed temporary rector," in 1707, and continued to officiate until 1719, occasionally repairing to the college at Saybrook and New Haven, but resided at Milford. "He was one of the ministers who assembled at Saybrook in 1708, by order of the General Court, for the purpose of adopting and recommending to the churches a manual of church discipline, called the 'Saybrook Platform.'" He died January 24, 1738. A daughter married the Rev. Timothy Cutler, who succeeded him in the rectorship of Yale College.—Sprague's *Annals*.

[31] (Wanting.)

[32] James Pierpont, who was born in New Haven, Conn., May 21, 1699, was the eldest son of the Rev. James Pierpont (Harv. 1681), the minister of New Haven, and Mary, daughter of the Rev. Samuel Hooker (Harv. 1653), of Farmington, Conn., and was graduated from Yale College in 1718. In 1722, he was elected tutor in the college, and was the first college officer to subscribe to the new tests of orthodoxy required by the trustees. Being senior tutor, he had more than the usual responsibility since there was no rector during his term of office. He resigned in 1724. A half sister of his married the Rev. Joseph Noyes (Yale, 1709), who succeeded his father as pastor in New Haven, and was one of the bulwarks of the "Old Lights." An own sister married the Rev. Jonathan Edwards (Yale, 1720), who became even more distinguished as a champion of the "New Lights." In the controversies of the period, Tutor Pierpont espoused the cause of the latter. He died in 1776. For the substance of this note, and for other facts, the editor acknowledges his indebtedness to Franklin B. Dexter, Professor of American History in Yale College. Professor Dexter

Note.   Mr. Andrew acted in y[e] capacity of a Rector by reason of y[e] vacancy y[n] made by Mr. Timothy Cutler,[33] Rector, who had declared himself an Episcopalian y[e] commencement before, together with y[e] tutor Mr. Brown[34] and sundry ordained ministers thereabouts.

Mr. James Pairpoint [Pierpont] and Mr. Will[m] Smith[35] were tutors. The colledge then consisted of about fifty students. It was erected at New Haven, in the year 1718; but first founded at Killingsworth, in the year 1702.[36]

At this colledge I tarried y[t] winter and had a chamber in y[e] colledge and chambered wth Gideon Southard [Southworth][37] my classmate, and was under the tuition of Mr. James Pairpoint —who was a better preacher y[n] scholar.

April, 1724.   This month I pay'[d] a visit to Boston from colledge and was allowed to studie that summer with y[e] Rev[d] Mr. Barnard, as heretofore.

---

generously placed in the hands of the editor, to be freely used, manuscripts prepared by him with great care, and after long and painstaking research, from which was derived much valuable information embodied in subsequent notes.

[33] Timothy Cutler was born in Charlestown, Mass.; graduated from Harvard College in 1701; ordained at Stratford, Conn., in 1709; married a daughter of the Rev. Samuel Andrew, and in 1719 succeeded the latter as rector of Yale College. Owing to a change of his religious views his official connection with the college was severed in 1722, after a brief three years of service. He immediately sailed for England, and received ordination at the hands of the bishop of Norwich, and also received from both Oxford and Cambridge the honorary degree of Doctor of Divinity. Returning to America, he became rector of Christ's Church, in Boston. He died in 1765, aged eighty-two.

[34] Daniel Browne was graduated from Yale College in 1714, and made tutor in 1718. His office was declared vacant in 1722, when, sharing in Rector Cutler's change of religious sentiments, he accompanied him to England for induction into holy orders, where he suddenly died of small pox.

[35] William Smith, one of the most eminent of the earlier graduates of Yale College, son of Thomas and Susanna (Odell) Smith, was born October 8, 1697, in Newport, Buckinghamshire, England. He was graduated in 1719, and in 1722, at a critical period in the history of the struggling institution, was elected junior tutor, continuing in office till 1724, when he resigned. On leaving New Haven, he repaired to New York, and is said to have been the only non-clerical graduate of any college residing in that city. He was at once, May 20, 1724, admitted to the bar, where he attained high distinction. "He was one of the early judges of the Supreme Court of New York, mayor of New York city, and prominent for many years in the conduct of the public affairs of the Colony." He died November 22, 1769. Prof. F. B. Dexter, *Manuscript Hist*, *Hist. Yale College, I*, 395.

[36] (Wanting.)

[37] Gideon Southworth is probably the person meant, Mr. Comer spelling the name according to its pronunciation. He was the son of Captain William Southworth, by his second wife Martha, and was born in Little Compton, then of Massachusetts, now of Rhode Island, March 21, 1706-7. He was graduated from Yale College with the class of 1727, and was afterwards settled in his native town, where he was married in January, 1727-8, to Priscilla, daughter of William and Judith Peabody. Upon her early death, he was again married, September 25, 1728, to Mary Wilbor, by whom he had several children

I have cause to mention ye name of that servant of ye Lord with the greatest honour and respect immaginable.

This summer a war broke out with ye Indians[38] while I was at Mr. Barnard's, which was a frontier town, and his house was garison'd, tho there was continual fear and a town watch or military watch rather, yet no hurt was done by ye Indians.

Sept. This month, in the beginning, I went to N. Haven to be there on the commencement and to tarry there till ye next spring, having spent the summer in private studie, which I esteem ye best.

A few days after ye commencement was over I was taken sick with a fevour which left me low, with a fevour and ague; upon which it was thought proper yt if I could go to Boston it would be better for me; soon after a sloop presented.

October 7. On ye back side of Cape Codd we were overtaken with an extreme storm of wind and rain attended with thunder and lightning in ye night wh did some hurt to our vessel, so yt none of us ever expected to see the light of another day; but through God's wonderful goodness ye next morning we were safely arrived in Plimouth Harbor.

Wednesd., 8.

Thirs., 9. We arrived safe at Boston.

Fryd., 10. This day Mrs. Rebecca Burnol exchanged this world for a better as I trust, and I was chosen a pall bearer and accepted. She was one whom I first fixed my affections on, and was truly a well accomplished woman, and noted for sobriety and virtue; but in her death the will of the Lord is done.

This sickness and trouble were motives to stir up my desires to obey Christ; but I seemed afraid, for I had told none my mind. Upon which yt word was made of a quickening nature to me, He that is ashamed of me and my ways, of him and his ways will I be ashamed *before my Father and the Holy Angels;* upon which I broke my mind to Mr. Callender in order to proceed in the month of December.

January, 1725. This day I was Baptized by the Revd. Mr. Elisha
Lord's Day, 31. Callender and was admitted into full communion with the Baptist church in Boston,[39] having before

---

[38] (Wanting.)

[39] The First Baptist Church in Boston was, according to the record, organized "on the 28th of the 3d month, 1665." The 28th of May, O. S., becomes 7th June, N. S. Among the early pastors were the following: Thomas Gould, Isaac Hull, John Russell, Thomas Skinner, John Emblen, Ellis Callender (1708–1718), Elisha Callender (1718–1738), Jeremiah Condy (1739–1764), Samuel Stillman (1765–1807), Joseph Clay (1807–1809). This list, with the exception of a single name, is taken from Benedict, who claims to have followed the

waited upon the Rev^d. Mr. Appleton, of Cambridge, and discoursed with him on ye point of Baptism, together with my resolution. Upon which he signified y^t I might notwithstanding maintain my communion in his church, by which I discovered ye candor and catholick temper of his spirit. He behaved himself ye most like a Christian of any of my friends at that time upon this account.

So I tarried in Boston y^t winter and resolved to go no more to colledge, but to follow my studies privately and to keep for a time a school in ye country if any presented.

April. Accordingly a school presented at Shewamet,[40] or ye lower end of Swanzey, and considering there was a Baptist church there, about 8 miles distant, I accepted ye motion.

Thirsd., May 6. This day I set out from Boston to Swanzey to visit ye church[41] and to keep school, if nothing hindered.

Church Manual of 1843. We have, however, ventured to insert the name of Thomas Skinner, on the authority of Mr. Comer, who says, in recording the ordination of Richard Dingley, which took place in 1689, as pastor of the First Church in Newport, "The ordination was by Mr. Thomas Skinner, pastor of the church in Boston, and Mr. James Barker, a ministering brother belonging to this church." There is a letter on record, sent from the church in Boston to the church in Newport, bearing date "ye 25th day of ye 11th month, 1679," which was signed by "Isaac Hull, John Russell, and Thomas Skinner, in ye name of the rest."

This church in Boston during all its earlier history maintained correspondence with the First Church in Newport and the First Church in Swanzey. When a disputation had been arranged by order of the governor and council between the Boston Baptists and their opponents, the First Church in Newport "hearing of this appointment, sent to the assistance of their brethren" a deputation, "who arrived in Boston three days before the dispute." —Backus, *History*, I., 301. The minute in the Records of the First Church in Newport reads as follows: "The Church at Boston Baptized upon profession of faith, being called by ye Magistrates to render an account of their faith together with their Pastor, Mr. Thomas Gold, on ye 14th and 15th of April, 1668, . . . this church not knowing but y^t they might meet with some difficulties, and so might want their help and assistance made choice of and sent down three messengers to them, viz. Joseph Tory [Torrey], William Hiscox, and Samuel Hubbard, who got there on ye 11th of April." When Mr. Bradstreet was chosen governor in place of Mr. Leverett, and their liberties were somewhat abridged, the church wrote to their brethren at Newport, 25th January, 1679, " that several of their brethren and sisters had been called to court, censured, fined twenty shillings apiece and to pay court charges," but the officers having the order to execute were not forward in the performance of their duty.

[40] The original tract of land which was granted to John Miles and his associates, and to which, in honor of the old home in Wales, they gave the name of Swanzey, "included," says Backus, "what is now Warren and Barrington, and the district of Shawomet, as well as the present town of Swanzey."—*Hist.*, I., 285; Baylies, *Memoirs of Plymouth*, II., 235.

[41] This church in Swanzey "is the oldest Baptist church in Massachusetts." Its founder, Rev. John Miles, "came with a colony from Swansea, in Wales, and settled in a section of what was then Rehoboth but subsequently was set off, and received the name of Swanzey." The Swansea church in Wales, which was organized in 1649, brought with it to this country in 1663 the old church records. There was a renewal of church relations in the new

Fryd., 7. This day about noon I got safe to Swanzey and went first as directed to the house of Deacon Richard Hardin—kindly entertained. At night I was conducted to Mr. Jonathan Kingsley's to keep as they had concluded. Sent back my horse by ye Post.

Saturd., 8. This day I visited the minister Mr. Ephraim Wheaton,[42] and was invited by him to preach ye next Lord's Day, which I accepted. Having been earnest with the Lord for ye bestowment of suitable gifts and graces for so sacred a service.

Lord's D., 9. This day I began my public ministry in the town of Swanzey, in the congregation and by the request of Mr. Ephraim Wheaton, Pastor of ye church of Swanzey, from those words, 1 Pet. 1 : 16, Be ye holy for I am holy, P. M. A large auditory. Thus I hope in the sincerity and uprightness of my soul, with a hearty and sincere aim to God's glory and ye advantage of precious souls, and under deep humility considering my own unworthiness I entered into ye work of the sacred ministry. Who is sufficient for these things. My grace is sufficient.

I continued to preach one part of ye Lord's Day by the request of ye minister.

June. This month I was invited by the town to keep the Public school, which I accepted, and for that service to have 44 pounds a year, tho I engaged only for one quarter.

July 30. This day I went to Boston to visit my friends and receive my portion.

Aug. 1. This day I was twenty-one years old.

Mond., 2. This day I received my portion of my Uncle, Capt. James Watson, and gave him suitable receipts; tho

---

Swanzey in the year of arrival. John Miles was pastor from 1663 till his death in 1683. Samuel Luther was ordained pastor in 1685, and continued his ministry till his death in 1717. Ephraim Wheaton, having been associate pastor from 1704, succeeded Mr. Luther in 1717. and continued in office till his death in 1734. This church maintained a correspondence with the First Church in Newport, and the First Church in Boston, and with the Particular Baptists of London.—Backus, *History*, II., 275, 433; Cathcart, *Bap. Ency.*

[42] Ephraim Wheaton was born in 1656. He served the Swanzey Church for thirty years, first as associate pastor with Mr. Luther from 1704 till the death of the latter in 1717, then as sole pastor till his own death, April 26, 1734. His meeting house, though in Swanzey, "stood near the borders of Rehoboth, and he and many of his people who lived therein were taxed to [support] Pædobaptist ministers of that town."—Backus, *History*, I., 500, 509. He occasionally corresponded with friends in London. Mr. Backus has preserved letters which passed between him and the munificent London merchant, Thomas Hollis. Letters of his are recorded in the books of the First Church in Newport. ["Elder" Wheaton appears to have been a valued friend of John Comer; they died within a month of each other, and were buried side by side.—J. W. W.]

in some things he dealt very disingenuously with me, yet I hope I can say I forgive him. Far be it from me to do otherwise.

Fryd., 6. This day I returned to Swanzey. At y⁰ church meeting the 5th of this month, the church chose five brethren to treat with me, to tarry and preach one year with yᵐ. I only preached before upon yᵉ request of yᵉ minister. The brethren appointed by yᵉ church were: Richard Hardin, deacon; Joseph Butterworth; Jonathan Kingsley; John West; Hugh Cole; who accordingly waited on me, but I refused because by some private action yᵗ I discovered I found some opposition to my settlement. So I did not promise any time, tho I concluded in myself to tarry a quarter with yᵐ. But finding a head like to be made and a positive vote in yᵉ church absolutely denied in a wicked manner by two or 3 persons who appeared free and easie to my face. Having been invited to Newport by Elder Willᵐ Peckcom's [43] congregation,[44] tho very small and low, I thought it advisable to go there, things having an ill countenance from yᵗ time to [this.]

---

[43] "Elder William Packcom [or Peckham, the name is variously spelled] was ordained to yᵉ Pastoral Office by the imposition of yᵉ hands of Mr. Samuel Luther, Pastor of the church in Swanzey, and Mr. Samuel Bullock, Deacon of yᵉ above sᵈ church, about yᵉ middle of November, in yᵉ year 1711"

A letter was sent, under date September 7, 1727, "From a church of Christ in Swanzey to a church of Christ at Newport under the care of Elder William Packcom and Elder Jno. Comer," "Signed by us yᵉ subscribers in behalf of yᵉ church,

HENRY SWEETING, Elder,
EPHRAIM WHEATON, Pastor,
JONATHAN KINGSLEY, Deacon.
HUGH COLE,
JOSEPH BUTTERWORTH."

"June 21, 1732, the church met at Elder Packcom's according to agreement. Brother Wm. Clagget began the meeting with prayer, yⁿ followed a discourse suited to yᵉ occasion, after which yᵉ Elders of yᵉ church imposed yᵉ hands on Brother Wm. Packcom followed by a prayer, yⁿ according to yᵉ desire of Elder Packcom we proceeded to Break bread, after which yᵉ antient Elder gave his good advice and Blessing to yᵉ church, and yᵉ meeting ended." Thus was set apart in a most solemn manner a brother to serve the church as deacon.—*First Church in Newport Records.*

Elder William Peckham married for his first wife a niece of Dr. John Clarke. He died August 2, 1734.

[44] The First Church in Newport, to which Mr. Comer now came, was at the time being sorely rent, and was consequently much weakened. Daniel White, who had come from England, and was engaged to assist the pastor, divided the church, and set up a separate meeting.

The organization of the First Church was effected probably early in 1638, the year of the settlement of the colony. Mr. Clarke began his ministry as soon as the colonists arrived. John Winthrop, the governor of Massachusetts, assures us of this fact in a written statement made that very year; in 1638 he affirmed that Mr. Clarke was "preacher to those of the Island." Thomas Lechford, "of Clements Inne," a cultivated gentleman who had traveled through the New England colonies, testifies in 1640, that "on the Island

Mond., Nov. 1. This day I went to Newport in order to live there if things could be made comfortable, having the day before preached my farewell sermon from Matt. 6 : 2.

In my going to N. port I followed yᵉ advice of Mr. Elisha Callender, Pastor of yᵉ Baptist church in Boston, bearing date Sept. 13th, 1725. These are some of the principal heads:

The first thing you have to do is to consider which congregation doth most of all want help, *i. e.*, Swanzey or N. port, and then where you may have yᵉ fairest prospect of doing good. These two things I think would determine me to go to Newport; and yⁿ besides some other considerations fall in which ought to have their force and they are these: Your own comfort in yᵉ benefit of conversation of wʰ to be sure there is greater choice at N. port. And yⁿ again as to your subsistence wʰ as far as I can learn is as like to be as comfortable at Newport as elsewhere; wᵗ other considerations you may have I know not; but upon yᵉ whole I pray God to direct you. But if you incline to go to Newport, I must advise you to these things: 1. To studie well all your public discourses and look upon it your business to compose sermons in a handsome style and good method; 2. Carefully avoid all controversies in yᵉ pulpit; 3. Be sure yᵗ you never enter into yᵉ contention⁴⁵ yᵗ has been at Newport. E. CALLENDER.

Mond., 13. This day I was called to Pastoral Office in yᵉ church by a unanimous vote.

Thirsd., Decembr 16. This day two men and a lad were drowned in yᵉ harbour between the fort and yᵉ town, yᵉ connue [canoe] in which they were sinking under them; yᵉ Lord's Day following I improved yᵗ word, Boast not thyself of tomorrow.

---

there is a church where one Master Clarke is pastor." Winthrop and Hubbard, in their histories, give concurrent evidence; when describing the rise of certain new religious opinions on the Island in 1639-40, they speak of Mr. Clarke as the accredited minister of a portion, at least, of the people on the Island; when the people became divided into two parties, these earliest historians say that from the new opinions broached, "their minister Mr. Clarke, . . . dissented, and publicly opposed" them. The early pastors of the church were: John Clarke (1638-1676), Obadiah Holmes (1651-1682), Richard Dingley (1688-1694), William Peckham (1711-1734), John Comer (1725-1729), John Callender (1731-1748), Edward Upham (1748-1771), Erasmus Kelley (1771-1784), Benjamin Foster (1785-1788), Michael Eddy (1789-1835).

At the time Mr. Comer became pastor of the church, its meeting house doubtless stood on Tanner Street (now West Broadway), opposite the small enclosed cemetery where Mr. Clarke lies buried. A meeting house was built on this site "in yᵉ year 1708 upon yᵉ lot of land which was given by Mr. John Clarke for yᵉ use of yᵉ church." The former meeting house was sold the year before, in 1707, which stood at "Green End."—Ross, *Hist. Disc.*; *Hist. of Ch.*; Cathcart, *Bap. Ency.*; Newport *Hist. Magazine*, IV., 71.

⁴⁵ Referring to the division created by Daniel White, who was at this time preaching to a party that had drawn off from the church.

January 1, 1726. This day I begin a new year. Since I have begun a new service I desire to go on in yᵉ strength of the Lord my God and to persevere unto my life's end.

Thirsd., 20. This day I changed my condition and entered into a married state with Mrs. Sarah Rogers [46] of Newport. I was married by Major John Coddington,[47] Justice of yᵉ Peace.

Lord's D. February 6. This day I gave my answer to the call of the church in the affirmative, to accept of yᵉ work of the sacred ministry among them.

Here follows an exact coppie of yᵉ answer delivered publicly in the face of ye congregation.

NEWPORT, Feb. yᵉ 6th, 1726.

Brethren and Beloved in our Lord Jesus Christ:

You have sometime since solemnly called upon the Lord of yᵉ harvest by humble and earnest prayer yᵗ he would send forth a labourer into this part of his harvest, such a one as might break yᵉ bread of life to you and dispense yᵉ living oracles of yᵉ holy one of Israel in this place.

Hereupon you were directed to make choice of the unworthy instrument who now reminds you hereof.

I trust Beloved you have deeply considered the awfulness of yᵉ call of a labourer to be improved in God's harvest; with yᵉ difficulties, discouragements, and temptations, such are exposed to. I have also seriously weighed, and humbly spread the case before the Lord, earnestly beseeching him to guide and direct me in so important and momentous an affair in being an ambassador for Christ to beseech sinners in his name and stead to be reconciled unto God. Hereupon I have considered

I. What the Lord Jesus Christ expects [from such] as preach the Gospel.

II. What men expect from them.

I. What the Lord X [Christ] expects.

1. Christ expects they should be faithful in it. 1 Tim. 1: 11, 12.

2. Christ expects they should keep close to, and not very far from, his commission to them. 1 Thess. 2: 2, 3, 4, 5.

3. They are accountable for all the acts of their office. Heb. 13: 17.

4. All such as are called are under obligation to preach yᵉ Gospel. 1 Cor. 9: 16.

5. Christ expects his word should not be corrupted to please men. 2 Cor. 2: 17. They should keep close to and not very far from his instructions in both yᵉ matter, manner, and end, of their ministry yᵗ so they may say as Christ did when sent, Jno. 7: 16: My doctrine isn't mine, but his yᵗ sent me; so St. Paul could say of what he delivered. 1 Cor. 11: 22, 23. So Timothy must keep what was committed to him. 2 Tim. 1: 14.

---

[46] [It is evident that this lady was not a widow. John Comer was her first husband. "Mrs." ["Mistress"] is used here and elsewhere, according to former custom, in speaking of single women of position in society. *E. g.* No doubt so of "Mrs." Rebecca Burnoll. See page 32. J. W. W.

[47] (Wanting.)

II. What men expect.

And here: *Men* expect y^t such should be examples to others in Doctrine, in Conversation, in Faith, in Purity.

I have also considered my own inability to perform these ministerial acts which are incumbent on those who are thereunto called,—of being the mouth of God's people to Him, and His mouth unto them,—of admitting into, and ejecting out of, his visible kingdom,—and of administering the Seals of the Covenant to his people.

But while I was musing and ruminating hereupon, y^t precious promise took deep impression on me, 2 Cor. 12: 9, My grace is sufficient for you; and y^t, Matt. 28 : 20, Lo, I am with you alway.

When I considered my small standing in ye School of Christ, the tenderness of my years, the smallness of my experience, the various temptations I am exposed to, and the greatness of ye work I am to engage in, I was almost discouraged. But considering the necessity of this flock of Christ,

Therefore Beloved in the Lord Jesus Christ, I now by the grace of God assisting me resolve to improve my utmost strength that God may afford me in this place by a compliance with your call to the work of ye ministry among you. This I do in ye name of the great God and the Lord Jesus Christ, in the presence of ye elect angels and this assembly, promising by ye help of ye Holy Ghost to perform ye ministry you have called me to, agreeable to God's word and your expectation, viz.,

To declare ye whole counsel of God and to keep nothing y^t I either do or shall know to be agreeable to God's will from you; and to administer the ordinances of the Gospel—Baptism and the Lord's Supper—as God has prescribed in his holy Word, without human alteration and unwarrantable tradition. So Brethren and beloved in the Lord X [Christ], I humbly beg your prayers to God for me to help and assist me in a work of so great importance which I should have laid before me, but the service of this afternoon hath made it sufficiently manifest to you.* So devoting myself to ye service of your souls, and ye souls of yours, in ye Gospel of Christ, whom I intreat through ye blood of the Everlasting Covenant to make you all perfect, stablish, strengthen and settle you, working in each of you y^t which, is well pleasing in his sight through Jesus Christ, to whom be glory in all ye churches world without end. Amen.

* NOTE.—I preached from 2 Cor. 2 : 16, Who is sufficient for these things.—JOHN COMER.

March 14. This day I had my Letter of Dismission and Recommendation from the church in Boston to the church in N. port. Signed in behalf of the church by

ELLIS CALLENDER,[48]
ELISHA CALLENDER, Pastor,
JOSIAS BYLES, Deacon,
EPHRAIM CRAFT.

---

[48] Ellis Callender, father of Elisha Callender and his predecessor in the pastoral office, was pastor of the First Baptist Church in Boston from 1708 to 1718. In 1714, Dr. Cotton

This day I was solemnly ordained by fasting, prayer, and the imposition of hands of yᵉ eldership, viz.,

MR. WILLIAM PECKCOM, Pastor,
MR. SAMUEL MAXWELL,[49] Deacon.

I preached myself that day from Matt. 28 : 20, Lo, I am with you alway. Mr. William Packcom gave me the charge, [which concluded with these words]: And in testimony of your reception to an equal part in yᵉ work of yᵉ sacred ministry, I give you my right hand.

The members of the church when I was chosen to yᵉ Pastoral Office were 18 in number, 10 men and 8 women.

There were at yᵉ same time in yᵉ town 7 places of public worship.[50]

Mather, pastor of the Third Congregational Church, addressed him a kind letter, breathing a very fraternal spirit, indicative of a changed attitude on the part of the "standing order" toward dissenting bodies. This letter is recorded by Backus in his History, I., 420.

[49] Samuel Maxwell became a member of the First Church in Newport, and was subsequently made a deacon of the church. His ordination to this office is thus recorded: "October 20, 1724, Peter Taylor and Samuel Maxwell were ordained by Imposition of yᵉ hands of Mr. Willᵐ Peckham and Mr. Ephraim Wheaton, pastor of yᵉ church of Swanzey, to yᵉ work and office of Deacons."—*Church Records.* Mr. Maxwell was dismissed to the Boston Church September 11, 1727, then returned and reunited with the church in Newport October 24, 1728, and was again dismissed, May 25, 1732, to the church in Swanzey. April 18, 1733, he was ordained colleague with the Rev. Ephraim Wheaton; "but he was unsteady in his sentiments, nd in 1738 he embraced the opinion of keeping the seventh day of the week as the Sabbath, which caused his dismission from the church, April 15, 1739." Backus, *History*, II., 434. In 1745, having retracted his opinions concerning the Sabbath, he took charge of a Baptist church in Rehoboth, but continued with them less than four years. A letter of his to Elisha Callender indicated other doctrinal defections. He "lived to a great age, and was esteemed a pious man; but he was so unsteady in his principles and conduct as to cause much unhappiness in the churches."—*Ibid*, 275.

[50] Callender says, in his *Historical Discourse*, "that there are at this time, seven worshiping Assemblies, Churches, or Societies, in this town [Newport], besides a large one of the people called Quakers, at Portsmouth, the other part of the Island." Page 120. In a letter sent from Newport to a gentleman in Dublin, Ireland, Dean Berkeley says, under date April 24, 1729, "Here are four sorts of Anabaptists, besides Presbyterians, Quakers, Independents, and many of no profession at all. Notwithstanding so many differences, here are fewer quarrels about religion than elsewhere, the people living peaceably with their neighbors of whatsoever persuasion." Quoted by Elton in his edition of *Callender's Historical Discourse*, p. 31. The Anabaptists, or the "Baptized Churches," as they called themselves, were divided into three distinct denominations. Besides the Regular Baptists, there were the Sabbatarians and the Six-Principle Baptists. The two former were Calvinistic in doctrine, the latter generally Arminian. The Free Will Baptists did not appear until very much later.

Doctrinal views were at this early period held with great tenacity. With the Six-Principle Baptists the imposition of hands upon all believers was a divine ordinance and binding on the conscience, and, equally with baptism, was a necessary pre-requisite to the communion.

Baptist churches. One under hands, [51] Mr. James Clarke [52] and Mr. Daniel Wightman, [53] Pastors. My flock, I being ordained a colleague with Mr. William Peckcom, Pastor. One 7th day church, [54] Mr. Joseph Crandall, [55] Pastor.

---

[51] "One under hands" designates what was afterward known as the Second Baptist Church, sometimes called the North Baptist Church. This was an offshoot of the First Church. "In 1652," says Callender, "during Mr. Clarke's absence in England, some of the brethren [of the First Church] embraced the opinion of laying on of hands, as necessary to all baptized persons, and in the year 1654 or 1656, the opinion [that] it was necessary to church communion and fellowship, together with their opinions of the doctrines of grace and freewill, occasioned some of them to separate, and form a church by themselves, under the leading of Mr. Wm. Vaughan."—*Hist. Disc.*, Elton's ed., 118. "These seceders," says Benedict, "objected against the old body: 1. Her use of psalmody; 2. Under restraint upon the liberty of prophesying, as they termed it; 3. Particular redemption; 4. Her holding the laying on of hands as a matter of indifference. The last article is supposed to be the principal cause of the separation."—*History* (1848), p. 467.

The early pastors of this church were, William Vaughan [1656-1677], Thomas Baker, John Harden, James Clarke, Daniel Wightman, Nicholas Eyres, Gardner Thurston (1759-1802).

This church became subsequently at one time very large, and numbered among its members many of the leading men of the town.

The first meeting house of the church was built on lands bought at two different times, the first part in 1697, the second part in 1703-4. It is the land on which the meeting house of this church at present stands. See notes 178½ and 187.

[52] James Clarke was nephew of Dr. John Clarke, and "ordained pastor of this flock [Second Church in Newport] in 1701, by the assistance of Rev. Messrs. Dexter, Tillinghast, and Brown, of Providence, and continued in good esteem until he died, December 1, 1736, aged 87."—Benedict, *History*, I., 501.

[53] "Daniel Wightman was his [James Clarke's] colleague and successor. He was born in Narragansett, January 2, 1668, was ordained in 1704, at which time he took the joint care of the church with Mr. Clarke. He continued in office until he died in 1750, aged 82."—Benedict, *History*, I., 501.

[54] This was "the first Sabbatarian church in America." In 1671 several members of the First Church, "entertaining conscientious scruples in regard to keeping the first day of the week as the Christian Sabbath, withdrew from the fellowship of that church, and organized themselves into a church." In the Records of the First Church there is "A brief and faithful relation of the Difference between those of this church and those who withdrew their communion from it with ye Causes and Reasons of the same. The brethren and sisters were: William Hiscox, Roger Baxter, Samuel Hubbard, Tacey Hubbard, Rachel Langworthy. Each of whom left ye church on ye 7th Day of December, 1671." This "Brief Relation" occupies nine closely written folio pages. The first pastor of the church was William Hiscox, who died May 24, 1704, aged 65. He was succeeded by William Gibson, who died March 12, 1717, aged 79. The next pastor was Joseph Crandall, who died in 1737.—Benedict, *Hist.*, II., 418; Ross, *Hist. Disc.*, 134. The original covenant of the church is given in Backus, Editor's Note, I., 325. The MS. of Comer containing it, and from which the editor of Mr. Backus' history obtained it is in the library of the Backus Historical Society. This MS. gives also the following item: "There was a Petition presented to ye Assembly of Rhode Island Colony by several of ye members of ye 7th Day Communion yt ye Market which was kept on ye 7th Day night be altered to ye 5th Day of ye week, which was granted May 2d, 1677."

[55] Joseph Crandall began his ministry in 1715 as colleague with Mr. Gibson, and at the latter's death succeeded him in the pastoral office, and continued in the same till his death, September 13, 1737.

One congregation under ye care of Mr. Daniel White. [56]
One Congregational church, Mr. Nathl Clap, Pastor, Mr. Bass y^t assisted him.
One Episcopal church, [57] Mr. James Honeyman, [58] Pastor.
One Assembly of Quakers, [59] very large.

---

[56] Daniel White came from the Rev. Edward Wallin's church in London, and with his family was received into the First Newport Church. "Mr. Daniel White, Elizabeth White, and Mary White were received by a letter from a church in Old England, May the 18th, 1718."—*Church Records*. He was soon invited to become an assistant to the pastor, the Rev. William Peckham, and succeeded in rending the church. The Records say, "Notwithstanding all ye advice given to heal ye unhappie division, the flock was divided; part held with their Ancient Pastor, and part with Mr. Daniel White, who was called to ye Pastoral Office on ye 7th of September, 1718, while ye whole were united, and by virtue of ye call without Imposition of hands, he Administered all ye Special Ordinances of ye Gospel." The rest of Mr. White's story is told in the following paragraph from the Church Records:

"Mr. White held up a meeting in ye town in ye Meeting House w^h was built for him in the year 1724, until ye 21st of July, 1728, which House he and Mr. Boyle sold to Mr. James Blackstock on ye 25th of June; and he took a farewell of ye place on ye 7th of August, 1728. Thus the meeting upheld by him finished - and ye only surviving member y^t he left behind him was a woman," a Mrs. Mary Hamblin. Mr. Blackstock afterward gave the building to the Congregational Church for a schoolhouse.

[57] "In 1700, after Quakerism, and other heresies had in their turn, ruled and tinged all the inhabitants for the space of forty-six years, the Church of England, that had been lost here through the neglect of the crown, entered, as it were, unobserved and unseen, and yet not without success. A little church was built at Newport, the metropolis of the Colony [in 1702], and that in which I officiate in Narragansett, in 1707."—McSparran, *America Dissected*. The Society for the Propagation of the Gospel in Foreign Parts, incorporated in 1702, sent two years later, in 1704, James Honyman as its missionary to labor in connection with this new church in Newport. The original founder of the church is said to have been S^{ir} Francis Nicholson, under whose auspices Mr. Dockyer, an Episcopal clergyman, gathered the church early in 1699 Besides receiving stated remittances from the mother country for the support of preaching, this church was frequently made the recipient of costly gifts from munificent friends. A meeting house having been built in 1702, "finished all on the outside, and the inside pewed well, but not beautiful," a bell for the same was received in 1709 from Queen Anne In 1733, Dean Berkeley gave the church an organ, and the same year Jahleel Brenton a clock for the steeple. The early rectors of the church were: Mr. Lockyer (1698-1704), James Honeyman (1704-1750), Jeremiah Leaming (1750-1760), Thomas Pollen (1754-1760), Marmaduke Browne (1760-1770), George Bisset (1771-1779). During the Revolutionary War the church was for several years without a minister.—Bull, *Hist. Trinity Ch.*; Arnold, *Hist. R. I.*, I., 559; *Newport Hist. Magazine*, IV., 7.

[58] James Honeyman was born in England about the year 1675, and was sent to this country as a missionary by the Society for the Pronagation of the Gospel in Foreign Parts, commencing his work in Newport in 1704. He made to the Society an annual report of his labors. These reports, continued till his death, contain a full history of his life. He died July 2, 1750, after nearly a half century of service in the same parish.

[59] "The rise of the religious Society of Friends appears from the most authentic data to have taken place in 1644," when "some piously disposed persons first associated themselves in religious profession with George Fox."—James Bowden, *Hist. of Friends in America*. In noticing the progress of the Society, Fox states in his *Journal*: "The truth sprang up first to us, so as to be a people to the Lord, in Leicestershire in 1644, in Warwickshire in 1645, in Nottinghamshire in 1646, in Derbyshire in 1647, and in the adjacent counties in 1648, 1649, and 1650, in Yorkshire in 1651." Staples, in his *Annals of Providence*, p. 420, says:

Aug. This month a hardened young man being committed to prison for theft, attempted to kill himself by stabbing an awl into his bowels, and to choke himself by tying his stockings straight about his neck, but was prevented. I being sent for about 9 of ye clock at night to pray for him, he appeared ye most awful spectacle yt I ever beheld, for I plainly discovered ye sad symptoms of a hard and obdurate heart. The next Lord's day I improved publicly that word, Job 41 : 24.

Septemr. About ye middle of this month one Hannah Suderick, a disconsolate young woman, as is supposed, drowned herself about 11 of ye clock at night. The town was alarmed by ye beat of ye drum (the ground why isn't certainly known). And in ye afternoon of ye next day one Catharine Cook attempted ye like action, but was discovered after she had fallen down in ye water; but upon examination before Edward Thirston [Thurston], Assistant, and Job Lawton, Justice of ye Peace, she seemed to be under ye power of Satan in a very awful manner.

On ye evening of ye Lord's Day between 8 and 9 of ye clock, towards the close of this month, appeared a very remarkable rainbow in the North west.

Novr. 27. This day, being Lord's Day, one Ruth Dennis a young woman about 17 years old, being at home in ye afternoon, was delivered of a bastard child, privately, and kill'd it and threw it into ye little house, by her own acknowledgement to me and ye rest of ye ministers of ye town.

28. Monday. This day I preached at New London, Mr. Stephen Gorton's[60] Ordination sermon, from 2 Cor.

"The first appearance of Friends in New England was in 1656. In July of that year two females of this denomination of Christians, arrived at Boston, from Barbadoes."

But the religious movements which led to Quakerism seem to have been earlier in this country than in England. This was one of the fruits of the Antinomian controversy which waxed warm in Boston in 1637, and drove a colony to the shores of the Narragansett. Soon after its arrival the controversy was renewed within its bosom. "There were those in Rhode Island who, as early as 1640, pushing still further the principle of the 'Antinomians,' went beyond the written word, and claimed to be in possession of an inner light, of a revelation from the Spirit supplementary to that of the Bible."—Barrows' *Development of Baptist Principles in Rhode Island*, page 40. Arnold, in his *History of Rhode Island*, I., 151, makes a similar affirmation. In consequence of this controversy of 1640 and 1641, some became "seekers," "who were afterward chiefly merged in the Society of Friends, and by their opponents styled Quakers." "When William Leddra and Marmaduke Stevenson came to Newport, in the year 1658 or 9, they found their brethren here."—Ross, *Hist. Disc.*, page 131. This Society subsequently became, in Rhode Island, very large and for more than a half century perhaps the most influential in the Colony.—Callender, *Hist. Disc.*, 120.

[60] This Stephen Gorton, who was ordained at New London, was a man of considerable

2 : 16, and assisted in conjunction with Mr. Jno. Moss and Mr. Valentine Wightman.⁶¹ There was a large auditory [audience].

<small>Decemr.</small> As to yᵉ blessing on my ministry this year I received to the table of the Lord, 24 persons; out of which I Baptized 19 myself from May 26th to Decemr yᵉ 23d. Yᵉ other five by other administrators.

This year one drowned, wilfully to appearance. One wilfully murthered her child.

What I had for support from my people this year, both from the church and congregation, amounted to £85 14s. 6d.

<small>January, 1727.</small> In the latter end of this month, on yᵉ Lord's Day A. M. several men went into a boat to attend a vessel bound to sea, and coming from yᵉ vessel near her side yᵉ boat overset and 3 men were drowned, (one of whom was a man which a little before was remarkably preserved 18 days in a long boat at sea with Capt. Moot). The other 3 were taken up alive by yᵉ ferry boat. One of yᵐ taken up alive was William Pinnegar. One of yᵐ drowned was Thomas Weeden.

<small>Fryd., 21.</small> This day I preached in prison to Ruth Dennis upon her request from Matt. 8 : 7.

<small>Mond. 31.</small> This day Mr. Hull, a stranger lately from London, came to visit me, having heard me yᵉ day before from Ezek. 33 : 11. He much faulted my sermon. He was a very strange-principled man, and upon discourse I found him a sad and dreadful *Antinomian*.⁶² He soon went to Boston.

---

gifts, and served in the ministry many years, "but he fell into some scandalous conduct, and his church was finally dissolved."—Backus, *Histo·y*, II., 517.

⁶¹ Valentine Wightman, descendant of Edward Wightman, who was condemned for his religious opinions at Litchfield, England, December 14, 1611, and burned April 11, 1612, was born in North Kingstown, R. I., in 1681. February 10, 1703, he was married to Susanna Holmes. Having been ordained in Rhode Island, he removed to Groton, Conn., about seven miles north of New London, in 1705, where he planted a church of the "Six Principle" order. Although this denomination of Christians was opposed to singing in their public worship, Mr. Wightman introduced it into his church, and defended the innovation with much ability in a pamphlet which was published. "Mr. Wightman's writings show that he was a student of the Scriptures and of the patristic writings, with a well balanced mind, of calm but decided spirit, of sound judgment, clear convictions, warm heart, plain and transparent speech, a wise man in laying foundations."—Cathcart, *Bap. Ency.* He continued his ministry at Groton for more than forty years, and died June 9, 1747, aged sixty-six years. He was succeeded in his pastoral office by his son, Timothy Wightman, who also filled the same for a period of more than forty years.

⁶² It is certainly "dreadful" when one imagines that the law of God does not concern the Christian, that it is not to be preached even as a rule of life; and "that the evidence of justification is to be looked for, not in purity of heart and life, but in a direct divine revelation." The reaction against Rome, which lay an undue stress upon works, upon mere rites, upon actions in their naked externality, drove some of the Reformers of Germany

Thirsd., Febry 2. This night about 12 of ye clock my first son was born, whom I named *John*.

Lord's D., March 19. This day I preached in Boston, A. M. for Mr. Elisha Callender from Numbers 23: 19. This is ye first time in Boston.

April 2. This evening a train of combustible matter was laid under the floor of ye Old Church porch, and set on fire, but was timely discovered so y^t little hurt was done by it. It was a very evil act.

6. This day Ruth Dennis was cleared by ye Court upon pleading not guilty, for want of evidence ye law required. She was guilty in the sight of God who sees. She was guilty in her own conscience by her frequent acknowledgments to me during her imprisonment, and I never (till she did) thought she would plead not guilty, all circumstances were so plain; but was not guilty in ye law. The judge of all the earth will do right, he won't clear ye guilty, not one guilty sinner shall escape his deserts.

May. This month the New English church[63] was first met in.

Lord's D., July 23. This day I preached at Swanzey from Phil. 1: 1, 2, being the first time after the trouble which arose about my invitation there to settle. Elder Ephraim Wheaton made an exchange with me and preached at Newport. Follow peace with all men; as much as lieth in you, live peaceably with all men.

---

into an equally erroneous position in the opposite direction. Antinomian tendencies appeared also among the Puritans of England under Cromwell. The controversy, earnest and intense, carried on in the New World in 1637, between two parties called respectively the "Legalists" and the "Antinomians," furnishes one of the early chapters of the history of the Massachusetts Colony, and was the immediate occasion of the settlement of the Colony of Rhode Island. It is well for us to remember, however, that neither the Legalists on the one hand, nor the Antinomians on the other, would admit all that their opponents respectively charged upon them.

[63] This is supposed to have been the Congregational church, of which Mr. Clap was pastor. This church had had a meeting house for many years. "In 1696, the first meeting house was built. It stood on a lot of land situated on the northerly side of Tanner Street (now West Broadway), between Edward Street and Green Lane. Here services were continued until 1720, with varied results."—T. W. Wood, *MS. Hist. of the Church*.

Neal, in commenting on the affairs of Rhode Island, in his *History of New England*, Vol. II., page 233, exhibits not only some prejudice, but not a little ignorance. Speaking of the first settlement of Rhode Island and its subsequent history, down to the period in which he wrote (1720), he says: "It was first inhabited by the Sectaries, who were banished from *Boston* in the year 1639, and has been the Asylum of such Persons ever since; but the Inhabitants now begin to be more civilized since there have been two Churches in the Island, one according to the *New English* Model, the other according to the Church of *England*."

28. This day was exceeding uncommon heat felt here and continued until Augt yᵉ 7th, many died with yᵉ extremity in some places.

Thirsd., Augt 5. This day Mr. John Adams⁶⁴ came to town to preach as an assistant to Mr. Clap.

Saturd. 7. This day my wife's father, Mr. John Rogers,⁶⁵ as I trust exchanged earth for heaven, suddenly. He was a serious and devout Christian.

24. This day our rightful sovereign, King George the 2d was proclaimed here; before which on yᵉ same day yᵉ funeral ceremony of King George the first was solemnized. He died June 15th before. All things on this occasion was performed with yᵉ greatest accuracy the circumstances would admit. On the Lord's Day following

Lord's D., 29. I preached from those words, 1 Kings 1 : 34, God, save King Solomon.

Saturd., Septemr 16. This day happened the strongest hurricane that hath been known it [here?]. It blew up trees by yᵉ roots in abundance; blew down several chimneys, and blew off yᵉ roof of a house, and blew sundry vessels on shore.

Mond., October 16. This day being invited (by a number of Baptists at Springfield⁶⁶ to pay yᵐ a visit, Mr. Elisha Callender, of Boston, having been there and on yᵉ 23 of July

---

⁶⁴ John Adams, son of Hon. John Adams of Nova Scotia, was graduated from Harvard College in 1721, went to Newport to assist Mr. Clap, and was the occasion of dividing the latter's flock. He was ordained pastor of a seceding body by a council which met on the 3d of April, 1728, the ordination taking place eight days afterward, on the 11th of the month. This pastoral relation was severed February 25, 1729-30, when Mr. Adams returned to Cambridge, where he died in January, 1740, aged 36. "He was distinguished for his genius, learning, and piety."—Sprague, *Annals Amer. Pulpit.*

⁶⁵ John Rogers, a member of the First Church in Newport, and also a deacon, was one of the signers of the deed, dated 3d day of March, 1707-8, conveying by sale the meeting house of the First Church, situated at "Green End," to John Vaughn. The names of those who signed "yᵉ deed on yᵉ behalf of the whole church" were, William Peckam, Thomas Rogers, William Way, Thomas Pecham, James Franklin, Joseph Rogers, Edward Smith, John Rogers. A letter sent by the First Church in Newport to the First Church in Swanzey, "April yᵉ 26, 1719," bears his signature with that of six others. At the time of the division of the church, caused by Daniel White, John Rogers went into the new organization; but at its dissolution returned to the church, of which he remained a member till his death.

⁶⁶ The letter of invitation "to yᵉ Church of Christ in Newport," was dated "Springfield, Sept. yᵉ 6th, 1727." "At a church meeting, October yᵉ 15th, 1727, information creadibly was given [the letter itself from Springfield to the church was for some reason delayed, and did not reach its destination till later] yᵗ a Number of Baptized Believers in Springfield had sent to the church for advice and assistance, that yᵉ minister might come up among them," etc., it was voted to accept the invitation and that the minister go thither to give counsel and help.—Cf. Backus, *Hist.*, I., 575.

before Baptized 11 persons) I set out on a journey for Springfield in company with Mr. Richard Hardin, [67] of Swanzey, [and] Mr. Thomas Russell, of Boston.

Wednesd., 18. In Plainfield my horse broke ye bridge and threw me off; but thro God's goodness' without any hurt to either.

Thirsd., 19. This day I arrived safe at ye house of Mr. Jno Devotion, at Southfield, being part of four days on ye journey.

Fryd., 20. Went over to Springfield and find all things agreeable. I wrote a journal of this journey distinct, yt I carried with me.

Lord's d., 22. Preached at Springfield from Acts 16 : 9, A. M., and Jno 17 : 3, P. M. 70 auditors.

Tusd., 24. This day Mr. Ebenezer Devotion [68] ye minister of Southfield came to see me and seemed much troubled about ye affair I came upon.

Lord's D., 29. This evening two ministers came to see me, viz. Mr. Devotion and Mr. Hopkins, and while they were with me, as it happened, the glorious God, who is a God doing wonders, as well as glorious in holiness, shook ye earth terribly. 'Tis ye most remarkable *Earthquake* ever known in N. England. It came on about 10 of ye clock in a calm night; it was universal through the whole continent. It awake many yt were asleep.

This night Oct. 29, 1727, is a night to be remembered and ye circumstances of it to be transmitted to posterity.

Moond., 30. This day set out for Newport, and lodg'd this night at Mr. Clap's, [69] who is ye minister of Wendom [Windham].

---

[67] It is uncertain whether or not this "Mr. Richard Hardin, of Swanzey," can be identified with the "Richard Hardin" mentioned by Backus in his *History*, II, 24, who in 1718 "became both a deacon and the clerk of the First Church in Swanzey." The rascality of Hardin was not discovered until 1730, three years after this journey was made by Comer to Springfield. This reference may be doing great injustice to Comer's companion on this occasion.

[68] This Mr. Devotion, minister at Southfield, or Suffield, son of John Devotion, was a native of Brookline, Mass.; was graduated from Harvard College in 1707; ordained at Suffield, June 28, 1710, and died April 11, 1741. A letter of his in connection with this movement at Springfield is given in Backus' *History*, I., 513–516. He married Naomi, daughter of the Rev. Edward Taylor (H. C., 1617), of Westfield.—Sprague's *Annals*.

[69] "Mr. Clap of Wendom," is probably the Rev. Thomas Clap of Windham, who was born at Scituate, June 26, 1703, graduated from Harvard College in 1722, at the age of nineteen, ordained as Pastor at Windham, Conn., August 3, 1726, where he continued until 1739, when, at the resignation of the Rev. Elisha Williams, he was elected, against the earnest protest of his devoted church, Rector of Yale College, and was inducted into office April 2, 1740.

Tusday, 31. This day we were lost in yᵉ woods and benighted at Warwick, very cold; but after some hours got to Mr. Jno Green's, lodg'd there this night. Snow fell a considerable depth.

Wednesd., November 1. This day in yᵉ evening got safe home thro God's goodness and found my family well. I bless yᵉ Lord for what experience of his goodness and presence I have enjoyed in my journey. The Lord prosper yᵉ intent. Mr. Jno Callender [70] preached in my congregation in my absence.

Lord's D., 5. This day I publicly improved on yᵉ account of the earthquake that word Acts 16 : 26, Suddenly there was a great earthquake.

Mond., 13. This day A. M. a boat was set over at Point Juda [Judith] with 4 persons on board. There being another boat in company, but could not help them, but got soon to town and inform'd, and with utmost speed a sloop went out, and about 8 of yᵉ clock in yᵉ evening found them lying on yᵉ side of yᵉ boat with yᵉ sea washing over yᵐ, having lain 7 or eight hours, and notwithstanding yᵉ coldness of yᵉ season and yᵉ extreme difficulties they were exposed to, thro God's goodness all were brought safe to town.

Wednesd., 15. This morning about break of day, a stranger newly from England who kept at Mr. Thomas Richardson's (who had been observed to labour melancholy) got out of bed and went down in his shirt and threw himself into the well, and was there found drowned.

December. This month one —— King, a workman at yᵉ Fort, going thither from yᵉ Point in a connue [canoe] which overset, and he was soon taken up dead.

This year proved troublesome to the state of this Colony, which was in a distressing condition. There never was so many supporters of yᵉ State taken away in one year as in this remarkable year. It looks like a sad token of God's displeasure. Major Holden, assᵗ, first of all about yᵉ month of December. The Hon-

---

During his presidency, which was highly advantageous to the college, and while the Rev. James Noyes was Pastor of the First Church (See Note 27), the college became involved in a long controversy which ceased only with the retirement of the President in 1766. The privacy into which Mr. Clap entered was of short duration, for he died in New Haven January 7, 1767.—Sprague's *Annals*.

[70] John Callender, who was to become the successor of Mr. Comer as pastor of the First Church in Newport, was now twenty-one years old, and had been out of college four years. He was a nephew of the Rev. Elisha Callender, was born in Boston in 1706, and graduated from Harvard College in 1723, having been educated on the Hollis Foundation.

orable Saml Cranstone,⁷¹ Governour, Ap. 26th. Edward Thirstone [Thurston] Ass^t, in ye same month.

At the Election in May the Honourable Joseph Jenks,⁷² Deputy Governour, was chosen Govr in Chief.

Mr. Jonathan Nichols, Ass^t was chosen Deputy Governour; he was called from his office by death in July following.

King George the first, July ye 15th, left his temporal [crown] and exchanged [it], I trust, for an eternal crown of glory.

This year is the most wonderful y^t ever I knew; this remarkable year 1727, in ye memory of man there never was such a one known here. In July, heat; in August, lightning; in September, wind; in October, earthquake; each of these in a very admirable manner. Four were drowned, accidentally, as some term^d it. One wilfully.

This year my ministry was crowned with some success, through the divine blessing upon it. I received to the Lord's table 7 persons, 4 of whom I Baptized, and 3 were Baptized by other administrators. What I had for support from my people, from the church and congregation, amounts to £93 12s. 4d.

Wednesd., January 17, 1728. This night Mary Dye went and drowned herself as the Jewry [Jury] gave it; but most concluded she was murthered by her husband. One of her arms was broke and on y^t arm appeared 10 black and blue stripes. She was not found until [*Sentence incomplete.*]

---

⁷¹ Governor Cranston died at the age of 68 years, having held the office of Governor of the Colony during the unprecedented period of twenty-nine consecutive years, being first elected in 1698. Arnold, in his *History of Rhode Island*, says, "He held his position, probably, longer than any other man who has ever been subjected to the test of an annual popular election."—I., 540. "In the strength of his intellect, the courage and firmness of his administration, and the skill with which he conducted public affairs in every crisis, he resembled the early race of Rhode Islanders. Thirty times successively chosen to the highest office, he preserved his popularity amidst political convulsions that had swept away every other official in the colony. He was the connecting link between two centuries of its history, and seemed, as it were, the bridge over which it passed in safety, from the long struggle for existence with the royal governors of Massachusetts to the peaceful possession of its chartered rights under the House of Hanover."—*Ibid.*, II., 83.

⁷² Joseph Jenks, as Comer spells the name in the text, and as he himself spelled it, or Jencks as given by Backus, or Jenckes as most subsequent writers have been accustomed to write it, was Deputy Governor of the Colony from 1715 until 1721, and again from 1722 until 1727, when at the death of Governor Cranston he was chosen as his successor, and held the office of Governor for the next five years, residing, at the request of the General Assembly, for most of the time in Newport. He died June 15, 1740, in his 84th year. He married Martha, daughter of John Brown, and granddaughter on her father's side of the Rev. Chad Brown, of Providence, and on her mother's side of the Rev. Obadiah Holmes, of Newport. A letter is preserved by Backus, in his *History*, II., 23, addressed by Governor Jenks while residing in Newport, to his pastor and brother-in-law, Rev. James Brown, pertaining to ecclesiastical affairs in Providence.

Fryd., 19. If she drowned herself 'tis concluded her husband's ill carriage was the cause.

Lord's D., 21. This day a separation was made in Mr. Clap's congregation on ye account of his refusing y^t Mr. Jno Adams should settle with him, and so Mr. Adams preached in ye school house [73] belonging to that society.

Lord's D., 28. This morning just about break of day a small speck of an earthquake was felt here.

Wednesd., March 20. This day I prayed with Elder Henry Sweating [74] being near the point of death,—at Rehoboth.

Thirsd., 21. This day I preached at Swanzey for Elder Ephraim Wheaton, it being ye day of public fasting throughout ye Province.

Fryd., 22. This day I prayed with Mary Bullock, at Rehoboth, being sick.

Tuesday, April 2. This day a number of Presbyterian Ministers [75] came to town to regulate ye affairs of Mr. Clap's congregation. Note. They set out from their respective homes ye day before upon which one y^t was for Mr. Clap said he remembered they set out to engage in ye work they effected *the first of April.*

---

[73] "Probably standing where the City Hotel now stands." Thomas W. Wood, *MS. Hist. of Ch.* In a private note to the editor, Mr. Wood says, "'The City Hotel' was the same hotel as is now called 'Park House.'"

[74] Henry Sweeting was an elder of the Swanzey Church. The officers of the early Baptist churches in this country seem to have been: 1. Pastor, 2. Elders, 3. Deacons. The Swanzey church having sent delegates to sit in the Council at Newport to examine into the alleged malfeasance of an "assign" of the John Clarke estates who returned without action was highly displeased on account of it, as the church's letter to Newport "dated June 4, 1719, witnesses; signed in ye Name and behalf of the Church,

By EPHRAIM WHEATON, Pastor,
HENRY SWEETING, Ruling Elder,
RICHABD HARDIN,
JOHN DEVOTION."
Newport Church Records.

See also note 43.

[75] The early churches of Massachusetts were essentially Congregational in their order, with, however, a strong flavoring of Presbyterianism. While every congregation contained within itself the power of self-government, every congregation or church had a board of elders or presbyters to which its discipline and government were practically committed. "A Government merely Popular or Democraticall . . . is farre from the practice of these churches, and we believe farre from the minde of Christ." (Richard Mather.) The power of church government we give "neither all to the people excluding the Presbytery nor all to the Presbytery excluding the people." This system found formal expression in what is known as the Cambridge Platform. [It may be questioned whether there is not here something worth thinking about.—J. W. W.]

E

Thirsd., 4. This day Mr. Eals [76] preached in Mr. Clap's pulpit from Gen. 32 : 26, 29.

Lord's D., 7. This evening a schooner from yᵉ Bay under yᵉ command of Capt. *James Emmit* in a mighty storm of wind accompanied with rain was cast on shore, on a sand beach at Westport, in this Colony, and all got on shore, being 6 in number (save one Indian girl who was drowned in yᵉ vessel); there were 4 Englishmen and one Indian. The 4 were so far spent with yᵉ difficulties of yᵉ storm, after they had travelled some distance from yᵉ wreck [that they] dropt down dead a little space from each other. Yᵉ Indian travelled a great part of yᵉ night till he found a hay stack, under which he sheltered till day, and yⁿ gave information so yᵗ they were all taken up and decently buried. Taken from Major Stanton's own mouth, of Westerly, who was the 2d person yᵗ came to yᵐ.

This day also Mr. Clap preached from Jer. 15 : 19, A. M.; Isa. 14 : 32, P. M., and did not invite of yᵉ ministers to preach. These texts were wonderfully adapted to yᵉ circumstances, and delivered in yᵉ audience of yᵉ council and messengers. Note, this was yᵉ last sermon he ever preached in yᵉ meeting house.[77] About half an hour after by yᵉ toll of yᵉ bell, Mr. Foxcroft [78] preached in yᵉ meeting house from Jno 17 : 11. I attended this meeting.

Mond., 8. This day yᵉ meeting house door was broke open, 'tis said Mr. Jno Coddington had yᵉ chief hand in it,

---

[76] Nathaniel Eals, or Eells, son of the Rev. Nathaniel Eells," was graduated at Harvard College in 1699; was ordained at Scituate June 14, 1704; and died August 25, 1750."—Sprague's *Annals*.

[77] "Father Clap" preferred to surrender his meeting house rather than his convictions of duty in this matter. Thomas W. Wood, in his *MS. Hist. of the United Cong. Ch.*, says: "On the evening of April 24, 1728, ' was another meeting of yᵉ Church (Second), wherein I proposed to them relinquishing the meeting house for Mr. Clap to return to it again, but was refused;' so wrote Mr. Adams. The First Church immediately commenced their second [third?] meeting house, which was finished in 1729, and stood on land deeded by Edward Pelham and son for the purpose on the south side of Mill street. This house was originally paid for partly by the First Church and congregation, and partly by monies raised by Boston ministers for the Second Church—the latter taking the old house on Tanner street [now West Broadway] and old sacramental furniture, and releasing the monies and parsonage to the former."

[78] Thomas Foxcroft was born in Cambridge in 1696, and graduated at Harvard College in 1714, and on the 20th of November, 1717, was ordained Pastor of the First Church in Boston as colleague with the Rev. Benjamin Wadsworth. When the latter was elected President of Harvard College in 1725, Mr. Foxcroft became sole pastor of the church, but two years later, in 1727, he received Mr. Charles Chauncey as his colleague in the ministry. Mr. Foxcroft was a warm friend of Mr. Whitefield, and ably defended him against the attacks of his enemies. He died June 18, 1769, "when he had lived nearly seventy-three years, fifty-two of which he had spent in the ministry."—Sprague's *Annals*.

yᵉ key being purposely laid out of yᵉ way. Mr. Baxter preached from Gen. 13 : 8. After sermon yᵉ result of yᵉ council in opposition to Mr. Clap was read publicly.

Thirsd., 11. Mr. Jno Adams was ordained over half Mr. Clap's church, *i. e.*, yᵉ Brethren, viz., Richard Clark, John Reynolds, Nathan Townsend, Randall Nichols, James Carey, Job Bissel, Ebenezer Davenport. The ministers who assisted were: Mr. Joseph Baxter,[79] Mr. James Brown,[80] Mr. John Webb, Mr. Thomas Foxcroft. About two hours after two of yᵉ ministers went out of town. There were two of yᵉ council yᵗ did not tarry till yᵉ ordination, *i. e.*, Mr. Eals, Mr. Billings.[81]

---

[79] "Joseph Baxter was born at Braintree, June 4, 1676; was graduated at Harvard College in 1693; was ordained at Medfield, April 21, 1697, and died May 2, 1745, aged sixty-nine. He published the Massachusetts Election Sermon, 1727." Sprague's *Annals*. He was Moderator of this Council.

[80] By a slip of the pen, we must think Comer wrote James for Richard. The record of this council, preserved in the books of the First Congregational Church, gives the name of Mr. Brown as Richard, and not James. "Richard Brown was born in Newbury, September 12, 1675; was graduated at Harvard College in 1697; was settled in the ministry at Reading, June 25, 1702; and died October 20, 1732, aged fifty-eight."—Sprague's *Annals*.

[81] The Records of the Second Congregational Church in Newport contain the RESULT OF THIS COUNCIL in the handwriting of the Rev. Ezra Stiles, which he transcribed while pastor of the church. The record is as follows:—

"A Council of seven Churches met by their Elders and Delegates in Newport in Rhode Island, April the 3d, Ann. Dom., 1728, at the desire of a considerable number of aggrieved Brethren of the Church and Congregation under the Pastoral care of the Revᵈ Mr. Nathˡ Clapp.

"After solemn supplication made to God for his gracious presence and Direction, and after a calm and strict Enquiry and the best Information we could possibly obtain both from the aggrieved Brethren of the Church and Congregation and others concerned, we come to the following Result unanimously agreed in Council upon mature deliberation :

"Altho' we could Thankfully commemorate and acknowledge the kind providence of our Glorious Lord in bringing the Reverend Mr. Clap to this place, making him the happy Instrument of Founding a Church here according to the order of the Gospell, and manifesting a gracious Presence of the Holy Spirit with him in the success of his labours; and therefore would honour him highly for his work's sake : Yet withal (after an impartial and thorow examination of the several articles of Grievance, which a number of his brethren have Exhibited to us in writing, a copy whereof we have given him, to which he refuses to give us any answer, tho often urged thereunto) We cannot but say we find sorrowful occasion to remark upon his want of a due Conduct in several late Instances which is matter of great grief to us, and we think Justly offensive to this [these] Brethren, and to the Churches of Christ—as

"Particularly, his refusing to Administer the Lord's Supper for the term of 4 years Together (notwithstanding the urgent desire of his Church and repeated Exhortation from his neighboring Brethren in the ministry) without giving any satisfactory reason, we judge to be very disorderly; a Reproach to our holy religion, and a breach of Solemn Church Covenant: For tho he hath sometimes pleaded bodily indisposition as the occasion of this neglect; Yet we think even in that case we may without any breach of Christian Charity say there was a want of due regard to the Institution of Christ, In that he did not Invite in the Pastors of some of the neighboring Churches who might easily have been ob-

These things I make a remark on that so I may take notice of ye working of Divine Providence in such a proceeding.

tained to Administer the ordinance in such a case of necessity; Especially when the brethren of the Church so earnestly Desired to Enjoy the precious Institution.

"Again, tho we find he has lately administered the ordinance and would rejoice in his being able to attend his Duty in that matter; Yet we think that even then he was faulty, and acted contrary to the rules of Christian Charity and prudence in administering it to a small part of the Brethren of the Church without giving at the first time . . . [*foot of page torn off, part of two lines*] calling in an Ecclesiastical Council to consider and advise upon the difficulties and differences in the Church.

"Again, his manner of admitting persons into the Church we find Exceptional in several Instances—Particularly, his taking in a woman very lately without proposing her publicly to the Church for their consent, is judged to be a violation of Gospell order, an unwarranted invasion upon the Liberty of the Brotherhood, and just matter of grievance to them.

"Further, as to his administration of the holy ordinance of Baptism, we find several things exceptional and very irregular objected against him, Particularly in the case of Mr. Randall Nicholls' child, and adult persons not being seasonably propounded.

"And then, as to his conduct with relation to the affair of Mr. Adams' Settlem^t as a colleague with him in the ministry, we Judge it in all regards to be very strange, and his refusing to Consent to the Vote of his Church and Congregation in that matter, without giving any kind of reason, carries with it the face of a reproachable self will'dness, and appears very plainly to be the unhappy means of that sorrowful Contention whereby religion suffers and order in the Church so much obstructed as at this day.

"We find that Mr. Adams hath received a Valid Call to settle in this ministry in conjunction with Mr. Clap by Virtue of the aforesaid Vote, tho not so regular in all its Circumstances: We cannot find by the strictest Enquiry made that any Just Exceptions are or can be offered against Mr. Adams' preaching or conversation: nor can we learn from the Brethren who have retracted their Votes (for Mr. Adams' settlem^t) that they are influenced by any other principle but a tenderness to Mr. Clap, and lothness to contradict and grieve him; And therefore the opposition which hath arisen, and is now carrying on to the Ordination of Mr. Adams (in pursuance of the call given him) is judged altogether unwarrantable, and without any sufficient grounds to support it.

"We find about ½ of the Church and Congregation are still very closely united in their affections to Mr. Adams, the Pastor Elect, and that his removal from Newport under the Circumstances of the present day is not at all likely to make for peace, nor will it have a Tendency to serve the Interest of religion in this place.

"Further, we think ourselves oblig'd to add, it appears to us that the notion of the aggrieved Breth's desire and design to drive away Mr. Clap is altogether groundless and untrue; they having unanimously expressed themselves, in presence of the Council, heartily willing to sit under Mr. Clap's ministry, if it may be with peaceable Enjoyment of Mr. Adams's ministry in conjunction therewith; and that they desire nothing more than . . . [*bottom of page torn off, part of two lines*] such measures in Church Government as are Generally practised in the Churches of New England, most agreeable to Gospel rule.

"We now in the name of our Lord Jesus Christ Earnestly Intreat and exhort Mr. Clap and the Brethren who oppose Mr. Adams' Settlem^t to consider these things in the fear of God, and Endeavor respectively a better regulation of their Temper and Conduct for the restoring lost peace and repairing the injured honour of Gospell order and religion. In particular, as uprightly Judging it the best and most prop^r Expedient for the end; We advise and beseech Mr. Clap and the Brethren to give their consent to the ordination of Mr. Adams, as a col'eague with him in the ministry, or give us forthwith some satisfactory reason (if any such they have in reserve) why they refuse it; or if they continue to refuse their consent, without rend'ring any sufficient reason for their conduct, and because we apprehend the ordaining Mr. Adams a colleague with Mr. Clap in the Pastoral Charge of one and the same flock, under the present circumstances against Mr. Clap's comfort, and

This is yᵉ second Congregational church in this Colony.⁸² The
the inclination of so great a part of the people, is not desirable: Therefore we advise the
aggrieved members to appeal to the Church for a release from their special bonds and
relation to them, and We desire the Pastor and brethren with him to give them a speedy
and loving dismission in order to their Embodying into a Distinct Church by themselves:
Which being done, we advise, that the New-formed Church, together with their associates
renew their call to Mr. Adams and invite him to take the pastoral care of them and if they
desire a speedy ordination, we cannot but Advise Mr. Adams to consent unto it.

"Further, it appearing to us, that the aggrieved brethren and their associates have in
their hands at least an equal interest and propriety in the meeting house with the others
concern'd, we therefore are of opinion, and our advice in this case is, that both churches
meet peaceably in the present house for Publick Worship; the Rev. Mr. Clap on one part
of the day, and Mr. Adams on the other, until another meeting house be provided by one
or other party, and a separation into two Distinct assemblies be amicably agreed upon.

"Moreover, in case Mr. Clap's adherents unreasonably reject the counsell given them, we
advise the other brethren notwithstanding to proceeed (with the help of some neighboring
ministers, whom we entreat to assist them if there be occasion) to Embody into a Church
State by themselves, and go on in prosecution of the advises above given, and we resolve to
afford them our best assistance as we have opportunity, for which end yᵉ agree and design
not to dissolve at present, but (by God's leave) to continue in being for some time.

"Finally, we commend the people of God with their Pastor and the other persons for
and with whom we are this day convened to the influence of Sovereign divine grace . . .
(*line gone from bottom of page*). And humbly beseech the God of all grace, to pour down
an healing spirit, for the restoring and Establishing brotherly love and serving the great
Interests of Christianity and Gospell order in this place.

"Thro' Jesus Christ our dear Redeemer to whom be glory and praise in the Church,
World without end, Amen."

JOSEPH BAXTER,
RICHARD BUNN,
NATHANIEL EALLS, } Pastors.
JOHN WEBB (Scribe),
THOMAS FOXCROFT,

JOHN CUSHING,
SAMUEL BASSET,
JONATHAN WILLIAMS,
THOMAS CHURCH, } Delegates.
GEORGE BARBER,
THOMAS NICHOLLS,
DANIEL HENCHMAN,

The Seven Churches, &c.
The first Ch in Boston, Revᵈ Thomˢ Foxcroft.
    Messenger, Mr. Jonᵃ Williams.
The Old Sᵒ Ch in Bᵒ, Mr. Daniel Henchman.
The New Nᵒ Ch in Bᵒ, Rev. John Webb, Mr. Samuel Basset.
The Ch in Reading, Rev. Richard Brown, Mr. Thomas Nicholls.
The first Ch in Medford, Rev. Jos. Baxter, Moderator, Deacon Barber.
The first Ch in Scituate, Rev. Nathˡ Ealls, Mr. Jnᵒ Cushing.
The Ch in Little Compton, Rev. Richard Billings, Mr. Thoˢ Church.

"Mr. Billings approved this Result, but rode home and did not assist in ordination out
of tenderness for Mr. Clap. The Result was probably read without his name. I have two
copies among the Church papers certified by the Council: [one] as this; in the other the
ministers' names are in their respective handwriting, and Richard Billings signed with his
own hand among the rest.   EZRA STILES, Pastor.
May 25, 1770."

⁸² Callender, in his *Historical Discourse*, in enumerating the churches in the Colony of

gatherers were some yt gathered ye first when Mr. Clap was ordained, which was Nov. 3, 1720, after he had preached here from ye year 1695.

Lord's D., 14. This day Mr. Clap began to preach in his own house,[83] had a considerable auditory.

Thirsd., May 28 This day my little son fell headforemost out of a back window in the lower room, about one P. M., about 5 feet high from the ground, and through God's goodness by ye administration of suitable means he was cured of ye wounds he received in his head in a little time. At first he was taken up for dead. O what cause of thankfulness I have for this favour.

Fryd., 31. About 3 P. M., one Deborah Grinman [Greenman] was kill'd with thunder, at Narraganset. There were some things remarkable in her death. Two nights before she dreamed yt a woman lay dead in ye same spot she was struck down in. She told her sister of it under great surprise, and yt she was kill'd wth thunder. In ye morning of ye day in which she was kill'd 'twas very clear, but she apprehended it would be a fatal day. And when ye cloud arose she said *there is yt which will do ye business*. Accordingly she was kill'd in ye same spot. She was burnt on ye side of her face, and her instep was broke. At yt time she had a child in her arms, which was stunned, but soon recovered.

Thirsd., June 13. This day my house was raised, and no hurt done by any of ye timber.

20. This day Mr. James Blackstock bought ye meeting house of Mr. Daniel White and Mr. Thomas Boyls. It was a very ill act, both in ye buyer and sellers.

Fryd., July 12. This day Governor William Burnet [84] arrived here in his passage to his government of ye Massachusetts.

Rhode Island, gives the Congregational as follows: Besides these two in Newport, "there are three Presbyterian or Congregational churches—at Providence, South Kingston and Westerly; each of them [being] supplied at present with a pastor, viz., the Rev. Mr. Josiah Cotton, at Providence; the Rev. Mr. Joseph Torrey, at South Kingston, and the Rev. Mr. Joseph Park, at Westerly."

[83] That is, in his own dwelling house, the parsonage.

[84] William Burnet, son of Bishop Gilbert Burnet (of Sarum), was born at the Hague, March, 1687, and named William in honor of the illustrious Prince of Orange. He came to this country in 1720, arriving at New York 19th September; was made Governor of New York and New Jersey; was subsequently transferred by George II. to Massachusetts. "As he was to pass through Rhode Island on the way to his new government, the Assembly voted him a public reception." On the 12th of July, 1728, "a ship of war from England brought Burnet, the new Governor of Massachusetts to Newport. Salutes were exchanged at the fort,

Tuesd., July 16. This evening about 8 of yᵉ clock there appeared in yᵉ North several streams reaching towards yᵉ zenith —continued about 3 qr. of an hour.

Through ye favour of Mr. Jnᵒ Coddington, this day I obtained yᵉ report of the council concerning Mr. Clap.

Lord's D., 21. This day Mr. D. White left off preaching in yᵉ meeting house. Here I would note that the trouble commenced between him and the church under my care in the year 1719, and a separation made; and in yᵉ year 1724, his meeting house was raised; it was first preached in April, 1725, in which month I was invited by Mr. White to preach there. His congregation broke to pieces in yᵉ year 1727; and in yᵉ year 1728, he sold it.

August 7. This day Mr. White left yᵉ town and went to Philadelphia.

Lord's D. 11. This day I preached in Boston, for Mr. Callender, from Jnᵒ 17 : 3.

23. This day a child was drowned at Connanicut.[85]

Wednesd., September 4. This day Capt. Clark and Capt. Elliot went by order of authority after a private schooner, who had done mischief, and committed robbery on *Gardner's Island*, but did no exploits.

Mond., 23. This day I removed into my house. The total for building cost £302 3s. 6d. The church gave me towards it £43 11s. 0d.

Wednesd., October 2. This evening about 7 appeared in yᵉ North a very wonderful light in yᵉ horizon for a considerable time.

Thirsd., 3. This morning about an hour before day, being in bed and awake, observing a very uncommon light I got up and finding it in yᵉ North, upon steady viewing at bottom of the horizon there appeared a thick vapour, and above it a redness like unto fire, and in yᵉ middle a hundred or more spears pointing upwards, extending towards the zenith. The whole body of yᵉ appearance had a slow motion towards yᵉ east, yᵉ whole face of yᵉ south was lighted as by yᵉ moon, which yⁿ had been set about 3 hours. The redness of yᵉ spears was not at all times of yᵉ same brightness, but constantly made a very awful

---

a public reception was given him, and the next day he proceeded to Boston."—Arnold, *Hist. R. I.*, II., 94, 96. Gov. Burnet died September 7, 1729.

[85] The name of this island, which lies in the Narragansett Bay opposite Newport, has been variously spelled: as Quononigutt, Quonaniout, Quinimicutt, Canonicut, Conanicut. It was early bought of the natives by the settlers of Aquidneck, along with Goat and Coaster's Harbor Islands.

show, the sky being in other places of a clear blue, and stars shining very bright.

Mond., 14. A sloop commanded by Mr. Wm Gardner with whom were Stephen and David Mumford, Peter Arault [Ayrault], and two Negroes, was lost as is supposed by a sudden storm of snow y^t arose. They went to receive prohibited goods brought from Holland, but did not do it.[86] It was ye first this year tho a very considerable one.

Wednesd., 16. This day I preached by request at Justice Thomas Church's house, at Little Compton, from Jno 17 : 3. Mr. Billings, the Presbyterian minister was present, and a large auditory.

Wednesd., 23. This day a Presbyterian church was gathered at Providence,[87] Mr. Josias Cotton[88] ordained Pastor.

About this time in ye month Mr. Joseph O'Hara, an Episcopal minister, came to Providence from England. After he had preached two or three days, on ye 3d he published himself to Mrs. Alice Whipple, of Providence. But before he was out, published news came y^t he was married, and in about 3 weeks his wife came. But he denied her to be so, by which he was defeated of his new intended match.

Lord's D., Nov. 3. 'Tis observed that ye last Lord's Day he preached in ye church, he was by an extraordinary gust of wind forced out of ye church in ye time of service. It blew in a large window at ye west end, and very much shook

---

[86] (Note wanting.)

[87] As was the case in Newport, so was it in Providence, Congregational preaching was maintained for some years before a church was gathered. From Judge Staples, *Annals of Prov.*, we learn that "a Congregational Pedobaptist society was formed about 1720"; and that "in 1723 the society erected a house for worship at the corner of College and Benefit Streets." "They had no settled minister until 1728," when Mr. Cotton came to them. On the day of his ordination a church was organized consisting of nine persons In 1770, "the Benevolent Congregational Society" was incorporated. The Society sold its meeting [house] in 1794, and built another "at the corner of Benevolent and Benefit Streets," which "was destroyed by fire on the morning of the 14th of June, 1814." The following year another house was erected upon the same site. The successive ministers have been as follows: Josiah Cotton (1728-1747), John Bass (1752-1758), David S. Rowland (1762-1774), Enos Hitchcock (1783-1803), Henry Edes (1805-1832). This became "the first Unitarian church in Rhode Island."—Arnold, *Hist. R. I.*, II., 77.

[88] Josiah Cotton, son of the Rev. Roland Cotton, of Sandwich, and great-grandson of the famous Rev. John Cotton, of Boston, was graduated at Harvard College in 1722, and ordained at Providence, October 23, 1728, "eighteen churches being present by their delegates to assist at the ordination"; the sermon on the occasion was preached by the Rev. Nathaniel Appleton; having been dismissed he was installed at Woburn, July 15, 1747; being a second time dismissed was installed at Sardown, November 28, 1759; and died May 27, 1780.—Sprague's *Annals*.

the whole house. The next Lord's day his people refused his preaching.

Tuesday 5. This day a man at Narraganset, digging a well, after he had dug 20 feet deep, it cav'd in upon him and kill'd. He was taken out next day.

Mond., 11. One Benjamin Douglass, in this town, being in drink, going into a little house fell down from ye seat and broke his neck—as the Jury gave it.

Lord's D., 17. This day I preached from 1 Tim. 4 : 6, and insisted on ye subject of Imposition of Hands on Baptized believers as such,[89] which people took occasion to be much offended at—but I refer the whole of this affair [to God].

Lord's D., December 8. A negro woman belonging[90] to Thomas Wickcom, was found dead in Dyre's swamp. She ran away ye day before.

Saturday 21. This day Mr. Joseph Carpenter, Mr. Linzie, an Indian and a Negro, were drowned in their passage from Hog Island to Bristol. The connue [canoe] in which they were, sunk under y^m.

This year has been a year of great exercise to me. I have been as it were in ye furnace of affliction. The difficulty in my flock has been heart wounding, and almost sometimes confounding, but I see God's grace is sufficient for me.

This year there were 6 lost, there were 6 drowned, accidentally, as some term it, one kill'd with thunder, one kill'd in a well, one found dead with his neck broke.

This year I received to the table of the Lord 3 persons, two of whom I Baptized, and one was Baptized by another administrator.

What I had for support from my church and congregation amounts to £38 0s. 0d.

---

[89] This sermon was the beginning of all the sorrows which Mr. Comer had with his church, to which he so frequently refers, and which were evidently deep and abiding. His heart was sorely wounded. The church in opposing what it conceived to be his erroneous notions, may not have exhibited the sweetest Christian spirit. Mr. Comer had embraced the opinion, held by the Six Principle Baptists, that the hands of the Eldership should be laid upon every believer when he enters the church of Christ.

[90] Negro slavery, and especially the slave trade, furnishes a dark chapter in the history of Rhode Island. "Barbadoes was the source whence Rhode Island received most of her slaves." In 1715, "Newport, 'as the metropolitan town in this colony,' received a grant of funds derived from duties upon imported slaves, for the purpose of paving the street leading up to the colony house." In the winter of 1728, the very season when the above entry was made in the Diary, the General Assembly "prohibited the manumission of any slaves, without sufficient bonds first given to the town for their maintenance by the owner, in case of their becoming disabled."—Arnold, *Hist. R. I.*, II., 96.

About this time I found my people so uncomfortable y^t we must divide from each other, which was exceeding grievous to me. The reason why I received no more from y^m this year was because they withheld *wickedly* what I was to have had justly by their own offer and former fulfilment because I preached up Imposition of Hands on Baptized believers as such (tho I made no bar upon y^t account), this, and this only was ye reason why they began ye quarrel with me.[91] So y^t all which I had from them for ye service of 3 years and two months, *i. e.*, from the 1st of Novr 1725, to the 1st of January 1729, amounts by the most exact account to £217 6s 10d

That is, in the year

1726,	£85	14s	6d	To building,	43	11	0
1727,	93	12	4	Small gifts,	26	.14	0
1728,	38	0	0				
	£217	6	10	Total, £287	11	10

Note that there are 35 persons more in the church y^n was when I came to the Island; 4 y^t I Baptized joined to Swanzey church who lived there. So that all y^t ever I Baptized are 29 persons; and 9 I received to special church communion who were before Baptized. The whole church when I came consisted of but 17 members, 10 males and 7 females.[92] There was no public singing till I came, and by ye blessing of heaven introduced it.[93] In ye time of my administration there was one excommunicated, Sept. 11, 1727; two set apart, one for drunkenness, one for disordered brain, Feb. 22^d, 1728. Three were as I trust thro grace translated to glory thro the gate of death.

Here I think proper to note the line on my father's side, and would on my mother's, but I don't know certainly.

My grandfather Mr. John Comer was born Apr. ye 26, 1644.

My grandmother Mrs. Elinor Comer was born July ye 20, 1644.

---

[91] Mr. Comer's language is very explicit, "this and this only was ye reason why they began ye quarrel with me." Some later writers have assigned other reasons for this separation of pastor and people. The church was certainly very reprehensible for attempting to withhold from its pastor the salary due him. No action on his part could warrant it in treating him with injustice, or even with discourtesy. Two members influential in the body were largely responsible for leading it into this wrong course.

[92] The Church Records say that "at ye time of ye Division in ye church [occasioned by Mr. White] there were in full communion 29 persons, 12 males and 17 females." Of these, ten "joyned in full with Mr. White in ye time of ye division."

[93] "Singing, which seems to have fallen into disuse, was re-introduced into the public worship." *Hist. of the Church*, p. 30. The church used "psalmody" in public worship as early as 1652, and without any doubt from the beginning.

THE DIARY OF JOHN COMER.

My father Mr. John Comer was born August ye 12, 1674.
My mother Mrs. Mary Comer was born May ye 26, 1680.
John Comer, Jr., was born August ye 1st, 1704.
Sarah Comer was born June ye 14, 1706.

Here I record the births of my children.
John the son of Jno and Sarah Comer was born Feby ye 2^d, 1726 or 1727.
Sarah the daughter of Jno and Sarah Comer was born Jany ye 8th, 1728 or 1729.
Mary the daughter of Jno and Sarah Comer was born June ye 14th, 1731.

By reason of building and my people beginning to be uneasie with me, I can safely and truly say, Only on ye account of my faith in, and public preaching of, ye doctrine of Imposition of Hands on Baptized believers as such, I was exposed to inconceivable difficulties; for w^t I expected to receive of y^m as I used to do, was in a very sinful manner withheld from me, so y^t I was forced to improve ye money I took up upon use to defray ye charge of building for ye support of my family, for I had but 38 pounds of y^m for ye last year, 1728.

Here I shall note the bonds I have given that so all things may appear clear, if I should not live to clear y^m.
Sept. the 5th, 1728, I gave Capt. Wil^m Peckcom a mortgage bond for 50 pounds y^t I took for me of ye Colony's money, for which I am obliged to pay annually 50 shillings; and the whole as ye Colony calls it in.
October the 14th, 1728, I gave sister Eliz^th Barker a bond for 40 pounds, to pay annually, £3 4s. 0d.
December the 31st, 1728, I gave Mr. John Odlin a bond for 50 pounds, to pay annually, £3 0s. 0d.
These bonds I entered into in the year 1728; so that all the use [interest] I paid this year was £8 14s. 0d.

Wednesd., Jan. 8, 1729. This day I and my people met at Elder Peckcom's house and I had a dismission by a vote from y^m to go to any church I thought proper.[94]

At about 12 of ye clock this night, my second child *Sarah* was born.

---

[94] Changed to 185½. (J. W. W.)

Thirsd., 9. This day I passed under hands by Mr. Daniel Wightman, and offered for transient communion until Spring, or till I saw how God in his Holy Providence might dispose of me.

Lord's D., 12. I preached in Mr. Wightman's congregation P. M. from Jnº 20 : 17. Mr. Samˡ Maxwell supplying my pulpit.

23. This day Dean George Berkeley [95] arrived here with his spouse and a young ladie in companie, in order to find a suitable place in America to settle a colledge; he was 4 months and 16 days to Virginia, where he made but a short stay; so to Newport he was 5 months. He is reputed a man of moderation.

Feb. 13. Being on Saturday evening a violent storm of snow attended with sharp lightning and hard thunder, which struck yᵉ west of yᵉ English Church broke 9 quaries [squares] of glass, melted yᵉ lead in sundry places, and in several parts of yᵉ windows it burnt yᵉ frame to a coal.

17. This day was found a number of persons in yᵉ act of counterfeiting yᵉ public bills of credit of this Colony.[96]

Here follows an exact coppie of yᵉ Articles drawn up by yᵉ money makers, who were discovered by Mr. Brown (who engraved yᵉ plate) Feb. 17, taken from yᵉ original by me thro yᵉ favour of yᵉ King's Attorney, Mr. Daniel Updike,

19. Feb. yᵉ 19th.

Whereas we, Nicholas Oatis, Samuel Hallet and David Richards, have unanimously joined in a firm League and Contract to use our best endeavors in our respective places to make and put off without discovery a quantity of paper money. In consideration

---

[95] Considering his brief stay in Newport, Dean George Berkeley made a profound impression upon the town. In pursuance of h's purpose to found at Burmuda, or at some other more suitable place in America, a college for the benefit of Indian youth, he arrived at Newport in 1729, where he intended to make his headquarters, and collect material for his contemplated institution. About two miles out of town he purchased a farm and built a house, which he called Whitehall. "Not far from his house, among what are known as the Hanging Rocks, is a natural alcove, which, opening to the south and roofed with stone, commands an extensive view of the ocean. Here tradition says that Berkeley wrote his 'Alciphron, or Minute Philosopher,' which was printed in Newport by James Franklin." The Dean was attended by a corps of literary men and artists, among them Smibert, who gave an impetus to American art. Soon after his arrival a philosophical society was formed, which somewhat later, in 1747, gave birth to the Redwood Library. Disappointed in his original purpose, he gave his farm to Yale College, and in 1731 returned to England. —Arnold, *Hist. R. I.*, II., 99; *Biog. Cyclop. of R. I.*

[96] To counterfeit these bills of credit had been declared felony by an act of the General Assembly.

thereof for a further proof and confirmation of our fidelity with respect to each other's safety, we have taken a solemn oath to observe and fulfill ye following Articles of Agreement made this 7th day of January, in ye 2d year of ye reign of George the Second, King of Great Britain &c Anno Domini 1728 or 1729. (1) That damnation shall be the portion of him or ym (let whatsoever punishment be inflicted upon them) who by speaking, writing, engraving, or any other way or means whatsoever, makes known or discovers anything of these our proceedings. (2) There shall none other be taken in as partner without ye consent and approbation of all concerned. (3) No one shall lay any claims to the plate and other materials thereunto belonging, but each of us shall have an equal share or part therein. Neither shall they be disposed of. (4) We Nicholas Oatis and Samuel Hallet oblige and bind ourselves jointly and severally to print and put off all ye bills we make yt the Companie shall judge passable. (5) I David Richards oblige myself to use my utmost skill to sign all that is made. (6) On demand ye Companie shall produce and give in an exact, true and faithful account of ye proceedings, and render to each one a third of ye produce or money received without reserving or keeping one penny to him or ymselves undiscovered to all concerned herein.

None shall put off or cause to be put off above 20s. per week without asking leave and getting a toleration granted by consent of all concerned. Any one shall at any time call ye rest to produce their money which shall forthwith be done; and in case there is found diminished of any one's due proportion above ye limited sum of 20s. per week without consent, he or they shall forfeit to him or ym yt stands clear of this agreement 50 pounds current bills of credit out of his or their own stock.

If anyone is betrayed or is imprisoned or meets with any other expense or trouble on this account ye Companie shall out of their particular stock, bear their proportion of ye loss in defraying of the charge and use all requisite means for his relief. God save ye King, prosper our progress herein, and keep us from all traitors.

Then each and every one of us taking ye Bible in our hands swore by ye contents thereof, to observe these Articles of Agreement and fulfil ye same, as witness our hands ye day and date before mentioned.

SAMUEL HALLET.
NICHOLAS OATIS.
DAVID RICHARDS.

E

P. S.—Whereas we, Hannah Hallet and Joanna Oatis, have been knowing to and concerned in ye foregoing Articles and our assistance (as heretofore) will be required to act in our husbands' absence in their stead and place, wh we promise faithfully to perform to ye best of our understanding, for ye interest, preservation and safety of ye Companie, and as there is none made privie to ye sd Articles of Agreement, we by ye above written solemn oath bind ourselves to secrecy not to declare on any account wtever anything contained therein, as also to observe and fulfil ye aforesd Articles in every particular, as witness our hands ye 23d day of January, 1728 or 1729.

JOANNA OATIS.
HANNAH HALLET.

Monday, March 3. A number of Baptists, Churchmen, and Quakers, in all 30 persons, belonging to ye township of Rehoboth, were committed to Bristol jail, by reason of their refusing to pay ye ministers' rate.[97] The measles brought into town, and spread.

Mond., 10.
Tuesday, 11. I went to visit ye prisoners at Bristol with Mr. Stephen Gorton. Upon ye request of ye prisoners I preached this day in ye old prison at Bristol, from Psalm 86 : 11. Sundry of ye town attended ye meeting. After meeting I returned home. Blessed be God.

I think to insert this account. The ministers of ye Episcopal church have some of ym received ye Primitive and Apostolical order of Baptism by a total Immersion in water. Mr. Usher[98] of Bristol in ye month of January 1724 or 1725 Baptized Mr. Carpenter of yt town. Mr. Piggot[99] of Providence in ye month of July 1726, Baptized Mr. Nathl Brown of Rehoboth his two

---

[97] Two others were added afterwards to the number of prisoners. A list of their names is given by Backus in his *History*, I., 518. "For refusing to pay that year's tax to John Greenwood and David Turner, ministers of that town, twenty-eight Baptists, two Quakers, and two Episcopalians, were seized and imprisoned at Bristol, by Jonathan Bisworth and Jacob Ormsbee, constables of Rehoboth; the main of them on March 3, 1729." "As no other way appeared of deliverance from a nauseous place which had injured their health, but paying said taxes and costs, this was soon after done by their friends."—*Ibid*.

[98] This was the Rev. John Usher, the second rector of the Episcopal Church in Bristol (then under the jurisdiction of Massachusetts), succeeding Mr. Orem about 1723.

[99] The Rev. George Piggot was sent by the Society for the Propagation of the Gospel in Foreign Parts as a missionary into New England; he first went to Stratford, Conn., in 1722; the following year to Providence, where he was settled over the newly formed Episcopal church, the first in Providence, and the third in the Colony. Gathered during the reign of the First George, it was in his honor called King's Church; in 1794, it received the name of St. John's Church.—Staple's *Annals of Prov.*

daughters and two men more together. Mr. Mack-Sparrow [100] [McSparran] of Narrowgansit [Narragansett] Baptized Mr. Chase of N. port on Rhode Island, in ye month of November, 1728.

Mond., 17. A man was found drowned at Capt. Mallbone's [Malbone's] wharf. 'Tis he was drowned ye December before: for a man was y^n misst from a vessel.

Mond., 31. This day Mr. Maxwell began to keep school. It won't last long, I believe.

April 3. This day I obtained this remarkable relation from Capt. Robert Gardner's own mouth, viz., A sloop bound from Newport on Rhode Island under ye command of Robert Gardner to ye Island of Antequa, who sailed thence on the 25th of September 1728, being in ye latitude of 23°. The night before ye wonderful salvation was wrought, w^h is ye subject matter of this relation, ye course being set South and by West, but they who stood at [the] helm varied a point and steered South South-West, and tho they were faulted for this variation, yet God so ordered it in his Holy Providence y^t they stood ye point, notwithstanding, w^h had they stood according to order they could not have discovered ye wreck, which God seemed to direct y^m to.

And not only so but ye night before ye discovery ye Capt was waked out of sleep 5 or 6 times by an uncommon dream of seeing strong men y^t were so broken y^t he could scarce understand y^m &c., which so affected him y^t he got upon deck under great concern of mind not knowing w^h it should mean. In ye morning about 7 of ye clock, he resolved to inform ye mate and going forward to do so, he espied about a league distant something floating on ye water. Upon w^h he ordered one to go to ye mast head; upon [this] he discovered men to be on board holding up a sail to y^m. This being on Wednesday, October ye 16th. Upon ye discovery whereof they made up to ye wreck and in about half an hour came up with her, and finding men on board, speedily got out ye boat and fetch't ye distress't persons, being 6 in number; upon which they related their sad condition unto y^m and by this information they found the wreck to be a sloop belonging to New

---

[100] The Rev. James McSparran, graduated at the University of Glasgow in 1709; came to this country in 1721 under the auspices of the Society for the Propagation of the Gospel in Foreign Parts, had for his field of labor the Narragansett Country, which embraced a very wide territory. He resided at South Kingstown, and ministered especially to St. Paul's Church, known sometimes as Tower Hill Church. In 1752, he wrote his tractate entitled *America Dissected*. He died December 1, 1757, "having been minister of St. Paul's (Tower Hill), in Narragansett, thirty-seven years."—Updike's *Hist. Narr. Ch.*

Haven in Connecticut, named by Mr. Samuel Miles of y^t place, who in September set out from thence bound to Antequa. Who upon ye morning of ye Lord's Day, Sept. 29th, just before ye day broke, being in ye same latitude in which they were found (for ye vessel lay like a log on ye water) ye wind being then at East South East and East N. E. blowing excessive hard, and ye sails furl'd, scudding before it; ye vessel ship't a sea which carried all upon deck over. We being 14 persons in all, 11 Whites and 3 Negroes, viz., Mr. Westbury, a passenger, his wife and two children, a son and a daughter, myself, 6 hands and 3 Negroes. At ye time of ye great seas breaking in there were 8 men upon deck w^h were washed away. It broke ye mast midway and ye waist of ye vessel, and carried away ye quarter deck, and broke in ye bulk head of ye cabin. Mr. Miles, Mr. Westbury, his wife and two children and a Negro were in ye cabin, 6 in number, upon which we got [y^m] upon deck as soon as possible (save ye Negro) who was supposed to be there drowned, and immediately a 2^d sea came and carried away Mr. Westbury's wife, but ye other hold were preserved (tho we were 4 in number); as soon as 'twas possible to recover sense after this sea, ye Master hearing a noise in ye water of some struggling (being just about day dawning), and finding 'twas two men who held by ye main sheet, all possible help was got for y^m and got y^m on ye hull of ye vessel wth y^m (there y^n being 6 in number) and finding ye vessel's stern sinking, with great difficulty by ye help of ye boom tackle fall (?) they all got to ye head of ye vessel. Y^e middle y^n being 3 feet under water and ye head only remaining about a foot out of water there they lay wth ye sea washing over y^m. And God who is a God working wonders found out a way for their preservation. Six sheep which were washt overboard swam to y^m and were a means to support y^m about one week.

Note, ye storm after it had continued about 24 hours abated and the weather as God ordered it was calm till ye night after they were taken up; which had y^t been so great as y^n to an eye of reason they had all perished. But with God all things are possible. With Prise (?) they got two hogsheads of water and some come out of a hogshead, and by ye water being over ye middle part of ye vessel a dolphin swimming in and lodged in ye sail w^h they had preserved, one of ye men catched it in his arms w^h help't y^m. And thus in this sad condition they remained often laying y^mselves down being wholly without expectation of ever seeing land again or having any longer time or opportunity of showing forth God's praises. But unexpected deliverance came after they had lain 17 days in ye deepest distress by a remarkable overruling Providence. On Monday, October ye 21, 1728, and thro God's goodness they anchored safe in Antequa, and Mr. Saml Miles and one more ye same day had an opportunity to [go] to N. York, and arrived there safe and had an opportunity to return to his house and show how great things ye Lord had done for him.

This relation I received from Capt. Gardner this 3d of Ap. 1729.

4. This day came up ye case of ye money makers to trial (save Saml Hallet who was at sea and D. Richards whose indictment had a flaw in it so y^t it was referred to ye next Sept court). Hannah Hallet was cleared. N. Oatis and his wife found guilty; he to pay 150 pounds and his wife 50, or be clipt.

This day also a vagrant person was whipt at ye cart's tail thro ye town for stealing.

Lord's D., 20. This evening about 10 of ye clock in ye Northern board [sky] appeared an awful light much like y^t, Oct. 3^d, 1728; one half towards ye West was very red and many flaming spears in it; and y^t part towards ye East was very pale and light, it had a slow motion towards ye East and continued some considerable time.

Mond., 28. Nicholas Oatis stood in ye pillory,[101] and had his ears clipt for making money. His wife's relations paid her fine. This is ye 2^d instance of this nature in ye Colony.

May 3. (Mr. White first met in his new meeting house in April 1725.) This day Mr. Maxwell left off keeping school.

Mond., 16. This day 3 years I was ordained to ye work of ye sacred ministry, the Lord grant me his grace to be faithful to souls, and help me to watch for souls as one y^t must give an account, Heb. 13 : 17. Chrysostom says, I remember, y^t that Scripture caused an earthquake within him and produced holy trembling in his soul. O y^t I may fear my remissness in y^e

---

[101] An old law requires each town to furnish itself with a pair of stocks wherein to secure offenders. While the fathers of the Colony provided for the citizen the largest liberty consistent with the public safety, they at the same time held that offenders against the public weal forfeited their liberty, and they did not hesitate to deal with them in a severe and summary manner. The modes of punishment—the whipping post, the stocks, the pillory, the clipping—adopted in several Colonies, were those then in vogue in England.

care of precious souls and may be excited to greater watchfulness. Yet Lord I hope I can say, if I know my own heart, I desire to do good to souls. And now since my circumstances are altered upon ye commotion in my flock, and since I stand at this day in no pastoral relation to any particular flock of Christ, ye Lord fit and dispose me for an installment over any flock where in his holy Providence he may cast me, either here or elsewhere, and grant me ye conduct of his Spirit y^t my ministry may be blessed for ye eternal benefit and salvation of many souls.

Lord's D., 25.   This day Mr. Samuel Maxwell left my flock and went to Church [Episcopal]. Strange doings.

June.   The first week of this month Mr. James Updike, of Narraganset, going in a small boat alone a fishing, being gone two days, ye boat was y^n found on ye backside of Connanicut and he in it dead. 'Tis supposed he fainted and so died, suddenly; for he had rolled up his line, and everything on board seemed as tho he had done and was returning home.

21.   This day came on ye Yearly Association here,[102] it is supposed to be ye largest Convention y^t ever hath been. There were present of ministers:

Mr. James Clarke (in ye 80th year of his age),
Mr. Daniel Wightman,
Mr. John Comer,
} of Newport.

Mr. James Brown,[103] of Providence.[104]

---

[102] This was the Yearly Meeting of the Six Principle Baptists, with whom Mr. Comer had identified himself. This Association must have held its annual meetings for several years; Mr Comer speaks of it as something well known. Knight, in his *History of the Six Principle Baptists*, p. 322, states that these Yearly Meetings began " about the close of the sixteenth century," he evidently means seventeenth century. The churches were represented in the Association by their elders and messengers.

[103] James Brown, son of John and Mary (Holmes) Brown, and grandson of the Rev. Chad Brown and of the Rev. Obadiah Holmes, was born in 1666, and married Mary Harris, granddaughter of William Harris, one of the five original settlers of Providence. The time of his ordination to the gospel ministry has not been recorded, nor the extent of his term of pastoral service. His sister, Martha, married Joseph Jenks, Governor of the Colony from 1727 until 1732.

[104] At the General Assembly held Tuesday, February 17, 1730-31, it was ordered, "forasmuch as the outlands of the town of Providence are large and replenished with inhabitants sufficient to make and erect three townships besides the town of Providence, and the land lies convenient," that such division be made.—*R. I. Col. Rec.*, IV., 443. The three towns thus created out of the "outlands" were Smithfield, Scituate, and Gloucester. The four churches in Providence mentioned in the text fell by the partition into different townships; one church being in Providence, whose minister was James Brown; two in Smithfield, the minister of the one Jonathan Sprague, and of the other Peter Place; the

Mr. Jonathan Sprague [105] (in ye 82 year of his age), of Providence.
Mr. Nicholas Eyres,[106] of New York.[107]

fourth church in Scituate, under the ministry of Samuel Fisk. Judge Staples, *Annals of Prov.*, 419, has fallen into a slight inaccuracy, in speaking of "one [church] in that part [of Providence] subsequently called Smithfield," inasmuch as there were two.

[105] Jonathan Sprague, son of William Sprague, of Hingham, was born in 1648.—Savage, *Geneal. Dict.* He lived in Weymouth, and fell under the censure of the General Court of Massachusetts, the sentence of court being passed against him in Boston, April 28, 1674; he then removed to Providence.—*Ibid.* If, as is probable, he can be identified with the Jonathan Sprague mentioned in the *Rhode Island Colonial Records*, he became somewhat prominent in the town of his adoption. He was admitted a freeman of the Colony of Rhode Island, May 3, 1681; served on a committee to adjust taxes in 1692; was deputy for Providence in 1699, 1700, 1703, 1706–1710, 1714; was in 1703 Speaker of the House, and member of the auditing committee.

Mr. Sprague was also a Baptist minister, and served as pastor of a church in Providence. He was a man of vigorous intellect, and wielded a trenchant pen. That he did not forget the treatment he had received in Massachusetts is made evident by a letter of his, dated February 23, 1722. This letter is given in full by Staples, *Annals of Prov.*, p. 434. Three Congregational ministers wrote to the authorities of Providence asking "whether the preaching of our ministers in Providence might not be acceptable"; and suggested "that a small meeting house should be built in your town to entertain such as are willing to hear our ministers." To this letter Mr. Sprague, in behalf of "the inhabitants of the town of Providence," made reply. An anonymous answer was printed at Boston, under date September 7, 1722, containing the action of the Court against Sprague. Mr. Sprague made rejoinder, January 24, 1723, stating that one of the witnesses against him "in that case at Boston, was afterward brought to repentance and joined the Baptist Church he belonged to in Providence."—Backus, *Hist.*, II., 9, 10. Mr. Sprague died in Smithfield in January, 1741, aged ninety-three years.

[106] Nicholas Eyres was born in Wiltshire, England, August 22, 1691; came to this country and settled in New York about 1711; the following year invited the Rev. Valentine Wightman to visit him and preach in his house; as a result of the preaching Mr. Eyres and a number of others were converted and baptized, and formed "a General or Arminian Church," and in 1728 built a house of worship on Golden Hill (Gold Street). In October, 1731, Mr. Eyres removed to Newport and became co-pastor with the Rev. Daniel Wightman, of the Second Church. After the death of the latter, he became chief pastor with Rev. Gardner Thurston as assistant, by whom, at his death, February 13, 1759, he was succeeded in the pastorship. Morgan Edwards says, Mr. Eyres "left behind him heaps of manuscripts, some polemical, some doctrinal, some political, for which he was every way qualified."

[107] A brief notice of this "Arminian Baptist Church" is given by Morgan Edwards; also by William Parkinson, in his *Jubilee Discourse*. When Mr. Eyres left the church it had already become "much broken"; "some of them," said Mr. Eyres, in speaking of the church, "deserted under a pretence of love to the principles of absolute election and predestination."—Backus, II., 29. The church soon after dissolved. The way was being prepared for another organization. About the year 1745, some who had been members of this church, together with others, formed themselves into a Calvinistic Baptist Church, since known as the First Baptist Church in New York City.

Long before these labors of Mr. Eyres, the place had been visited by two stalwart Baptists from Newport, Obadiah Holmes and Samuel Hubbard, possibly on a missionary tour. Hubbard says, "Brother Obadiah Holmes and I went to the Dutch and Gravesend, and to Jamaica, and to Flushing, and to Hamsted, and to Cowbay, 1st October; came home 15th November, 1657."

Mr. Valentine Wightman, of Groton.[108]
Mr. Philip Tabor,[109] of Dartmouth.[110]
Mr. Stephen Gorton, of New London.[111]
Mr. Daniel Everett,[112] of South Kingston.[113]

Mond., 23. Met this morning at Mr. Wightman's house, 32 persons in all, viz. 8 ministers, 3 deacons, 21 brethren. There are of churches in communion 13 distinct bodies. In Providence, besides those above mentioned there are two under ye care of Mr. Peter Place [114] [and] Mr. Samuel Fisk.[115] In y^e

---

[108] This was the first church of this order in Connecticut, gathered about 1705. The two Wightmans, father and son, filled the pulpit of this church for a period of more than eighty years. This church gave name to the Association known as The Groton Conference, formed at a much later date.—Backus, *Hist.*, II., 414, 510, 516.

[109] Elder Philip Tabor was with others imprisoned May 25, 1723, "in the common jail at New Bristol," where he remained for thirteen months, for refusing to pay the tax assessed by the town for the support of the minister of the "standing order." A petition in behalf of the prisoners, drawn possibly by Mr. Tabor, was presented to King George, and an order was granted for their release.—Backus, *Hist.*, I., 500. Mr. Tabor died November, 1752.

[110] The genesis of the Dartmouth Church was as follows: "John Cooke, whose name we meet with on the first and on nearly every page of the early records of the town, as a deputy and a selectman, filling various offices of trust and honor, was a Baptist minister for many years."—*Old Dartmouth Centennial*, p. 86. Mr. Cooke had been connected with the church in Plymouth, but embracing Baptist views had become a member of the First Church in Newport. He labored as a preacher "in Dartmouth many years, from which labors," says Backus, *Abridgement*, p. 135, "sprung the Baptist Church, in the east borders of Tiverton." Of this church in Tiverton, Benedict says, *Hist.*, I., 503, that it "was formed in the adjoining town of Dartmouth about 1685; the members at first lived in Dartmouth, Tiverton, and Little Compton." Mr. Tabor was the third pastor of the church. Having removed its "seat from Dartmouth to Tiverton," says Benedict, "it continues to the present day," and has since been known, says the editor of Backus, "as the First Baptist Church in Tiverton, R. I."

[111] This church at New London, the second of its order in Connecticut, was formed November 28, 1726; but after a few years it was "dissolved."

[112] Elder Daniel Everett continued to serve the church until his death "soon after 1750."

[113] This church existed "as early as the year 1725." S. F. Hancock, in a *Historical Sketch of the First Baptist Church of South Kingstown (Wakefield)*, says: "Knight, in a statement of doubtful accuracy, places its origin in 1680 (Knight's *Hist.*, pp. 278, 319). Benedict follows Knight. Other indications point to a date later than 1710." About the year 1750, "Elder David Sprague, from North Kingstown, who had changed from 'general redemption' to 'particular,' disseminated the latter views in the church. Divisions ensued, and the church finally became extinct. Isaac Backus, writing in 1784, says that it had then 'long been dissolved.' "—*Ibid.* See also *Centenary of the First Baptist Church in South Kingstown* (1881), a pamphlet of 91 pp.

[114] Peter Place, of Providence, perhaps son of Peter, of Boston, swore allegiance to Charles II. in May, 1682.—Savage, *Geneal. Dict.* Knight is certainly in error when, having spoken of the death of Jonathan Sprague, he says: "Elder Peter Place succeeded him, and perhaps was his colleague."—*Hist.*, p. 267. He evidently confounds two distinct churches, both in Providence, and at the time of the division, both were set off with that part called Smithfield.

[115] Knight, *Hist.*, p. 270, says, Mr. Fiske was ordained in August, 1727, and died about 1744. This church, at the time of the division of Providence, fell into the new town called Scituate.

town of Swanzey one under ye care of Mr. Joseph Mason.[116] In ye town of Warwick one under ye care of Mr. Manassah Martin.[117] In North Kingston one under ye care of Mr. Richard Sweet.[118] 'Tis supposed there were 250 communicants and 1000 auditors. Each of these held ye Doctrine of Genl Redemption.[119]

There are 3 other churches y^t hold ye Doctrine of Free Grace.[120] One at Newport under ye care of Mr. William Peckcom, formerly my flock. One at Swanzey under ye care of Mr. Ephraim Wheaton. One at Boston under ye care of Mr. Elisha Callender.

There are two churches in ye observation of ye 7th day.[121] One

---

[116] This church " was formed upon different principles from the first, and they held the laying on of hands upon every member as a term of communion, and did not sing in their public worship," says Backus, naming some of the distinguishing characteristics of the Six Principle Baptist churches.—*Hist.*, II., 434. Preaching commenced in 1680, was continued until a church was formed. " Thomas Barnes was ordained their pastor in 1693," and the relation was continued until his death, June 8, 1706. His successor, Joseph Mason, brother of Samson Mason, a soldier in Cromwell's army, was ordained pastor "in July, 1709, and continued so till he died, May 19, 1748," at the age of almost ninety years.—*Ibid.*

[117] This church was formed " and Mr. Manasseh Martin was their minister before 1730."—Backus, *Hist.*, II., 511. It was probably formed not long before this Yearly Meeting. John Hammett was an assistant pastor from 1744 until his death in 1752.—Knight, *Hist.*, 274. Mr. Martin died March 20, 1754.—*Ibid*, 275. The earliest records of this church that have been preserved commence in 1741.

[118] The earliest records of this church reach back to 1710. The church was, however, doubtless gathered at a much earlier date, as " Elder Thomas Baker, one of the first pastors of the Six Principle Baptist Church in Newport, soon after his ordination removed to North Kingston, and raised up a church in that order."—Knight, *Hist.*, 265; Backus, *Hist.*, II., 505. Knight says: " In 1710, Richard Sweet was ordained their pastor, and continued to serve them with zeal and usefulness for many years, and deceased about 1740." Mr. David Sprague was ordained a colleague with him about 1739.

[119] This term, "general redemption," is liable to be misunderstood; it does not mean " universal salvation," but " unlimited atonement " ; it was sometimes employed to represent that system of doctrine known as " Arminianism." This was the doctrinal status of the churches in New England known as "Six Principle Baptists." Whether this Arminianism was of the so-called New England type which Dr. Park (*Associate Creed of Andover Theol. Sem.*, by Edwards A. Park) considers Pelagian or Semi-Pelagian, or of that type commonly considered as within the limit of the term " evangelical," like that of the Wesleyans later, does not come within the scope of our present investigations. It is more to our purpose to say that these churches about the time Comer was making the above entries in his Diary were multiplying rapidly and becoming quite numerous, especially in Rhode Island. But a decade later, when there appeared " the great awakenings in other parts of the country," these churches were strongly affected.—Backus, *Hist.*, II., 505 Many of them were dissolved and others became Calvinistic in doctrine, and renounced the " laying on of hands," at least as a necessary prerequisite to the communion.

[120] These churches were Calvinistic, emphasized the doctrine of Election, and made prominent the sovereignty of God in the work of salvation. At a later period, under the labors of Whitefield, the number of these churches was greatly multiplied.

[121] " In the beginning of 1665, Mr. Stephen Mumford, a Seventh Day Baptist, arrived from London at Newport, and Mr. [William] Hiscox, Mr. [Samuel] Hubbard, and other members of Mr. Clarke's church, soon embraced the keeping of that day."—Backus, *Hist.*, I., 324. See also note 54. The Sabbatarian churches were Calvinistic in doctrine.

at Westerly under yᵉ care of Mr. Joseph Maxson.¹²² One at Newport under yᵉ care of Mr. Joseph Crandal.¹²³

In all of Baptist churches in New England, there are 18 in number.¹²³¼

---

¹²² Westerly was first settled by colonists from Newport, some of whom were members of the First Church. "Hopkinton was once the north part of Westerly, where some of Mr. Clarke's church lived, before the separation on account of the Sabbath took place in 1671. Mr. John Crandall was one of them, who was imprisoned with Clarke and Holmes at Boston, in 1651."—Backus, *Hist.*, II., 506. At the time of the division in the church, the brethren at Westerly embraced the views of the Sabbatarians. In 1708, these brethren formed themselves into a church there. Frederic Denison, in his *Westerly and its Witnesses*, p. 60, says: " The organization was formed when the town numbered but 580 inhabitants, in 1708, under Rev. John Maxon, Sen., as pastor, and is still existing as the First Hopkinton Seventh Day Baptist Church. Their first meeting house is believed to have been built 'about the year 1680,' and was located on a lot given for that purpose by Peter Crandall." The first pastor was succeeded by his son, John Maxon, Jr.; the latter was succeeded by Joseph Maxon, "son of the first and brother of the second pastor." He was born in 1672, ordained in 1732; on the death of his brother in 1742 he succeeded to the pastoral office, "though seventy-five years old"; he died in September, 1750.

¹²³ This church, which was formed in 1671, had for its first pastor William Hiscox, until he died, May 24, 1704, aged ninety-six, when he was succeeded by William Gibson, from London, who was pastor until he died, March 12, 1717, aged seventy-nine. Joseph Crandall, who had been his colleague for two years, was chosen his successor, and remained in office until his death, September 13, 1737. Backus, *Hist.*, II., 502. Benedict confounds this Joseph Crandall with John Crandall who was fined in Lynn in 1651.—*History*, II., 419.

¹²³¼ [In examining Dr. Barrows' papers I found the following extracts copied from the Records of the Second Church, Newport, which may be a matter of interest as embracing historical facts concerning that church and also concerning an Association which I suppose was composed of "Six Principle Churches"—which churches appear to have had "general meetings" at an early date. *See* Note 102.—J. W. W.]

I. Extract concerning the Second Church, Newport.

"Ch meetings first held Dec. 31, 1726, for attending to business of the ch. An accᵗ of the time when members were admitted into the ch for yᵉ year 1716 taken from brother Timothy Peckhom's note book by reason of there being then no stated record kept by yᵉ voice of the ch, transcribed this 8ᵗʰ day of March, 1729—here is an accᵗ of yᵉ receipt of members 10 years before yᵉ ch appᵈ a Record."

1716, Dec. 10. WILLIAM CLAGGET.
 Jan. 4. ELIZABETH BARKER.
  She removed abᵗ a year later to the other Baptist ch. [Comer's writing.]

"The land on which yᵉ meeting house now standeth made over to yᵉ church by Mr. James Clarke, pastor, who obtained yᵉ deed thereof in his own name October yᵉ 23ᵈ, 1697, in which year the first meeting house was built." [JNO. COMER.]

"To all Christian people to whom this present instrument may come I James Clarke of Newport on Rhode Island in yᵉ Colony of Rhode Island and Providence Plantations &c. sendeth greeting.

"Know yᵉ yᵗ whereas I sᵈ James Clarke did buy or purchase a certain piece of land lying and being in yᵉ town of Newport aforesᵈ containing 30 foot from North to South and from East to West and is bounded Easterly on a highway Northerly and Westerly, on Nathˡ Coddington's land, Southerly by a piece of land left out for a highway, all which lot or land was bought by me sᵈ Clarke of Major Nathˡ Coddington together with all yᵉ rights and privileges thereunto belonging as is set forth more at large and will more fully appear by yᵉ deed thereof bearing date October 23, 1697.

"Also another piece of land containing 30 foot in length and 40 foot in width and part of

| July 14. | This day Mr. John Adams and I waited on Dean George Berkeley at his house. Kindly treated. |

s⁴ purchase is a certain gore containing 8 foot in breadth and is butted and bounded Northerly on s⁴ Coddington's land, Easterly on highway and land already in possession of s⁴ Clarke and Westerly on land of s⁴ Clarke's and Southerly on a way, as may more fully appear by a deed dated Mar. yᵉ 23, 1703 or 1704.

"Know yᵉ yᵗ I James Clarke do hereby declare and publish yᵗ yᵉ money yᵗ did purchase both pieces of land was contribution money given by certain brethren hereafter named to build a meeting house on, for the worship and service of God, and for the accommodation of yᵉ same. (Jeremiah Clarke, Danˡ Wightman, John Odlin, John Greenman, James Brown, John Hammet, Jeremiah Weeden, Joseph Card, James Barker, William Rhoos, Stephen Hodley, Timothy Peckhom, Peleg Peckhom, Danˡ Sabear, Joseph Weeden, William Greenman, Henry Clarke, John Rhodes.)

"In witness I have hereunto set my hand and seal this 23ᵈ day of Jan'y 1706 or 1707.
JAMES CLARKE.

"Witnesses: { JOHN OSBAND, ELIZABETH WILLIAMS.

"Personally appeared before me this 6ᵗʰ day of February 1706 or 1707 James Clarke yᵉ subscriber hereof and did own and acknowledge yᵉ above writtten instrument to be his act and deed.   Attested, JOHN ROGERS, Justice of peace."

II. Concerning the General Meetings and Association.

"We the Elders and Messengers of several Baptist Churches met at Providence on the 22ᵈ 23ᵈ and 24ᵗʰ days of June 1764 have agreed to drop the General Meetings at Providence and Swanzey, and to set up an annual association of the Baptist Churches in Rhode Island Providence Plantation and the adjacent parts in manner following:

"1. The Association to be held annually on the 3ᵈ Thursday in May at the town of Providence.

"2. Every church to depute three brethren to represent them at the association under the names of messengers whereof one shall be an elder, these messengers to be chosen by the church, or the major part thereof at a meeting properly convened for that purpose.

"3. Each church shall prepare a letter addressed to the association wherein the names of the messengers shall be mentioned, the state of the church shown with reference to the number of members at the time, the number added that year, the number dead, and the number excluded, and if the church should labour under any difficulty, so as to want the advice, opinion, or help of sister churches, that the difficulty or case be fairly stated in their letter; Provided always yᵗ no matter be referred to the association which may be settled by the church itself.

"4. The association to be formed and conducted in the following manner: (1) To begin with public service at two o'clock on the day above said, the person to preach the associational sermon (and in case of his failure another) to be nominated at each association, so that he or they may have notice a year beforehand. (2) A moderator and clerk to be chosen before any business to be entered upon. The office of the moderator will be to direct and maintain decorum. The office of clerk to enter the names of the messengers, make minutes of the transactions of the association, and keep the association book. (3) The association shall draw up a letter directed to the several churches whom they represent, and a copy thereof shall be sent to each church, wherein everything shall be specified which concerns the churches to know in a way of information or advice.

"Signed in the name and behalf of the general meeting at Providence, June 24ᵗʰ, 1764, by

The Elders: { JOB MASON. GARDNER THURSTON. CHARLES HOLDEN. REUBEN HOPKINS.

"At the association held at Providence May 16, 1765, ordered that the association for the future be holden on the first Thursday in June."

18. This day Mr. Joseph O'Hara,[123½] ye Church priest, at Providence, was conveyed to jail here for his breaking open ye door of ye church, wʰ his people had fastened up after they had hauled him out of his pulpit on ye 9th instant for his irregularities.

Mond., 21. This day a meeting house was raised for Mr. Clap's congregation.[124] Also this day I gave Madam I. Cranston a note for twenty pounds I had of her.

Tuesd., 22. I went to Providence; accompanied my mother as far as Rehoboth. Lodged at Justice P. Tillinghast's.

Thirsd., 24. } I went up into ye woods to see Mr. Jonathan
Fryd., 25. } Sprague, 15 miles; preached in ye woods at Mr. Sprague's meeting house,[125] from 1 Tim. 1 : 14. A considerable auditory.

Saturd., 26. Returned to town.

Lord's D., 27. This morning Mr. Cotton sent a note to invite me to preach for him in ye forenoon; but I could not gratifie him. Preached at Providence in Elder Brown's congregation. This morning I received a letter from Mr. O'Hara and his commission signed by Edward Gibson (formerly Bishop of Chichester, translated thence to ye See of London, now in ye 7th year of his translation), dated at Whitehall July ye 1st, 1728.

The land to build ye church on was given by Mr. Nathˡ Brown of Rehoboth, ye deed bears date, Sept. 18, 1722; ye church was built 1724.[126]

The Baptist, Presbyterian, and Quakers there, about ye same time built.

Mond., 28. This evening was an awful and total eclipse of ye moon.

Tuesd., 29. I returned from Providence, got home yt night well. Blessed be ye Lord. This day a young man was drowned near Castle Hill.[127]

Fryday, August 1. This day I am arrived to ye 25th year of my age. O yt I may have understanding to improve my time to God's glory. I this day heard Mr. Adams from Ps. 26 : 6. Make yt my resolution.

[123½] This unworthy man is called Charro by both Staples and Updike. They both mention that he was dismissed from his charge for highly improper conduct.

[124] This house was built on Mill St. See Note 77.

[125] What Mr. Comer here calls "the woods," the General Assembly in dividing Providence describes as "the outlands of the town." See Note 105. Knight says this meeting house stood "about one mile north of the Smithfield Academy."

[126] (Wanting.) [127] (Wanting.)

Lord's D., 3. — This day Elder Peckcom administered yᵉ sacrament of yᵉ Lord's Supper to my former flock, yᵉ first time since last October.

Fryday, 8. — This day Mr. O'Hara visited me and gave me a coppie of yᵉ result of a Justice's Court concerning him. Here follows yᵉ Coppie: At a Court of Justices held at Providence for his Majesty this 2ᵈ day of August, 1729, present, Richard Waterman, Assistant, Ezekiel Warner, James Dexter, Justices of yᵉ Peace; to make some inquiry into a complaint yᵗ was laid before us by the Revᵈ Mr. Joseph O'Hara concerning the abuse that was done him in the church, in sᵈ Providence, on yᵉ 9ᵗʰ day of July last past, and how the church doors are fastened against him; and he producing before us a Commission from under yᵉ hand and seal of yᵉ Honorable yᵉ Bishop of London to execute yᵉ office of a minister in Providence during his pleasure. Whereupon our opinion is yᵗ if his complaint be proved by evidence as he hath laid it before us, it was barbarous usage; and the church doors being fastened against him is illegal and contrary to his Majestie's interest. Whereupon this matter is referred to yᵉ Court's next sitting for a further inquiry and hearing.

Saturd., 9. — Heard Mr. Hiscox from Ecc. 12 : 1. He instanced yᵗ yᵉ time of youth was yᵉ best time—(1) For good impressions; (2) for strongest resolutions; (3) for fixed affections; (4) for closest applications; (5) for diligent observations. He added further yᵗ not to remember God in youth was—(1) To slight his invitations; (2) disregard his legislations; (3) disbelieve his imprecations; (4) to reject his opperations. He finely run thro yᵉ chapter tho very briefly to my great satisfaction.

Lord's D., 10. — Preached all day, Mr. Wightman [being] at Narraganset. Mr. Hix's son's funeral bid to. Blessed be yᵉ name of yᵉ Lord for strength afforded.

Mond., 11. — Visited sundry of my hearers.

Tuesd., 12. — Began to transcribe Mr. Pardon Tillinghast's [128]

---

[128] Pardon Tillinghast was born in England in 1622; came to this country in 1645, settling it is said in Connecticut; but the following year he took up his residence in Providence, for his name appears among purchasers of land in 1646. *Annals of Prov.*, 61. He married Lydia, probably a daughter of Philip Tabor, of Tiverton, Savage, *Geneal. Dict.*, and was mentioned in 1672 as "a leading man among the people called Baptists, at Providence."—Geo. Fox, *Pub. Narr. Club*, V. 320. At what time he became pastor in Providence is not known, but "it was during his ministry, and after the church had lived without one for more than sixty years, that we first hear of a meeting house which was built at his expense, and given by him to the church in a deed dated in 1711."—Caldwell, *History of First Baptist Church*, 9. In the deed, "he describes the faith and order of the church to be the same as that now held by the Six Principle Baptists."

judgment in ye Revelation. He was pastor of ye Baptist church in Providence;[129] I had it of Elder Brown.

Having been moved heretofore to speak in publick of these things which are mysterious, which none but they to whom it is given can understand w^t ye Spirit saith unto ye churches:

1. The opening of ye first seal, showeth by ye going forth of ye white horse ye powerful conquest made by ye glorious gospel of Christ in ye days of X [Christ] and his apostles, ye weapons of their warfare not being carnal, but mighty thro God to ye pulling down of strongholds to ye obedience of Christ, this victory and ye effects of it were famous for 2 or 300 years after X [Christ].

2. Ye 2^d seal by ye coming forth of ye red horse, showeth ye bloody wars that arose in ye earth and chiefly at Jerusalem, ye next generation following and ye dreadful persecution of ye saints foretold by X [Christ] Matt. 24, and also to his faithful church of Smyrna in chap. 2, ye shall have tribulation 10 days, meaning 10 reigns of cruelty.

3. Y^e 3^d showeth by ye black horse and his rider wth ye balance in his hand, ye coming forth of grievous wolves foretold of, y^t would make merchandize of ye word, seeking their gain from their [every] quarter and greedy of filthy [lucre], contrary to X [Christ] and his apostles' commands and examples, then begun and still continued by pretended ministers even to this day and darkness of these times.

4. Y^e opening of ye fourth seal under ye pale horse and his rider, w^h was death and hell following, showing the dead and woful condition ye professors of ye gospel were now come into, as ye word mentioned chapt. 16, the 2^d angel poured out his veyal [vial] on ye sea, and it became as ye blood of a dead man, and every living soul died in ye sea, the bottomless pit now being begun to be opened and ye smoke darkening ye sun and air.

—*Annals of Prov.*, 414. Although Mr. Tillinghast received no pecuniary compensation for his services as pastor of the church, he maintained his right to receive such compensation. Governor Joseph Jenks, writing from Newport, under date March 19, 1730, says: "I believe there are several of my brethren who can remember that Elder Tillinghast (in his lifetime), who was a man exemplary for his doctrine, as well as of an unblemished character, did several times in his teaching declare that it was the duty of a church to contribute towards the maintenance of their elders, who labored in the word and doctrine of Christ; and although for his own part he would take nothing, yet it remained the church's duty to be performed to such as might succeed him."—Backus, *Hist.*, II., 23. Mr. Tillinghast died January 29, 1718, at the age of ninety-six years. See letter of Moses Brown, on "The Descendants of Pardon Tillinghast," in *Newport Hist. Mag.*, Vol. III., pp. 156-162.

[129] (Wanting.)

5. Ye 5th seal showeth ye bloody work of ye scarlet coloured beast and of the whore of Babylon yt was drunken wth ye blood of ye saints and martyrs of X [Christ], whose blood cryeth for vengeance agt their abomination of desolation.

6. Ye 6th seal showeth ye ruin and desolation of ye churches' enemies after their iniquity is come to ye full, their sun, in wh they so gloried, should be black like sackcloth of hair, and their moon, stars, and all ye host of their heaven, their greater and lesser lights, shall flee as a scroll, by reason of ye earthquakes and shaking yt shall fall upon yt wicked state, and all ye supporters thereof: when ye Lord shall arise to shake terribly ye earth, Isa. 2, and this concurs wth ye pouring out ye vials of wrath. Chapt. 16.

7. The opening of ye 7th seal, showeth ye saints ye rest promised after their long and great sufferings of tribulation, according to yt [word] of St. Paul to ye Thessalonians, [tribulation] to ym yt trouble you, and to you who are troubled rest with us; when ye Lord shall be revealed from heaven with his mighty angels in flaming fire. There is silence in heaven. Rest and quietness after so many exercises. Then is ye Lamb's book of life opened. Rev. 6.

Thirsd., 14. Transcribed out of Mr. Clarke's Narrative.[130] Mr. John Clarke,[131] Mr. Obadiah Holmes,[132] and Mr. John

---

[130] Of this work, printed in London, "by Henry Hills, living in Fleet Yard, next door to the Rose and Crown, in the year 1652," only one or two copies are extant. It has been once republished, and may be found among the collections of the Massachusetts Historical Society, with this prefatory note: "The manuscript from which the following reprint is made was transcribed from a copy of this rare tract in the exceedingly valuable collection of works on America, belonging to John Carter Brown, Esq., of Providence, R. I.; which copy was kindly loaned to the Society by the owner for the purpose for which it is now used."—4 *Mass. Hist. Coll.*, II., 2.

[131] John Clarke was born in Suffolk, England, October 8, 1609; was educated at one of the English universities; emigrated to this country in 1637; was the leader of the colonists that settled Rhode Island; was imprisoned and fined in Massachusetts, in 1651. It is to this visit that reference is made in the text. Mr. Palfrey, in his "History of New England," finds a political motive in the visit. Dr. H. M. Dexter, in his monograph, "As to Roger Williams," follows suit. For reply, *see* pamphlet, of 49 pages, entitled, "Early Baptists Defended," by H. M. King, D. D.; also an article in Baptist Quarterly, Vol. X., pp. 353 seq., reviewing Dr. Dexter's book. Besides being almost constantly employed in the public service to guide the infant commonwealth in the midst of its manifold difficulties, Mr. Clarke was a preacher of the gospel, and was so engaged from the very first year of the settlement of the colony even until his death, during this long period serving the First Church as its faithful and devoted pastor. See further, Note 152.

[132] Obadiah Holmes was born in Preston, Lancashire, England, about 1606; came to this country about 1639, settling in Salem, Mass.; six years afterward he removed to Rehoboth; thence in 1650 or 1651 to Newport, R. I.; was imprisoned, fined, and whipped in Massachusetts, in 1651; he was pastor of the First Church from 1652 until he died, October 15, 1682; was buried upon his own farm in Middletown, the spot being marked by a simple slab.—Cathcart, *Bap. Ency.*; Sprague's *Annals*.

Crandal,[133] were taken up by ye Justice of Lin [Lynn], Mr. Robert Bridges, there on y^e Lord's day, July 20, 1651, and committed to Boston jail for being Baptists, and on y^e 31 of July had the sentence of Court passed on y^m, y^e 1st to pay £20 or be whipt, y^e 2^d £30 or be whipt, y^e 3^d £5 or be whipt. None suffered but Mr. Holmes, and y^t in a terrible manner to y^e extent of y_e law. Mr. John Wilson,[134] a Presbyterian minister, struck Mr. Holmes when he went from y^e bar and said, *The curse of God go with thee.* He died Oct. 15th, 1682.

The first free school in N. England was in Charlestown, founded in 1635.[135]

---

[133] John Crandall, the third of the trio, who went to Lynn in 1651, and suffered imprisonment, was an elder in the First Church, and died about 1676. He was spoken of by Samuel Hubbard, in a letter to the Rev. Edward Stennett, in England, as "my dear brother John Crandal."

[134] John Wilson was born at Winsor, England, in the year 1588; came to this country in 1630, in company with John Winthrop, and became "teaching elder" of what was afterwards known as the First Church in Boston; in 1632, he was chosen pastor, and the Rev. John Cotton the following year became his colleague as teacher, this relationship continuing until the death of the latter in 1652, when in 1656 the Rev. John Norton became teacher. Mr. Wilson was again left alone by the death of Mr. Norton, in 1663, and so continued until his own death, August 7, 1667. He was the leader among the opponents of the Antinomians in 1637; his colleague Mr. Cotton inclined to the other side of the question then disturbing the good people of Boston.—Sprague's *Annals.*

[135] The honor of having established the first free school in New England has been claimed for Newport. On the 20th of August, 1640, the town of Newport voted to call Mr. Lenthall "to keep a public school for the learning of youth, and for his encouragement there was granted to him and his heirs one hundred acres of land, and four more for a house lot"; it was also voted "that one hundred acres should be laid forth, and appropriated for a school, for encouragement of the poorer sort, to train up their youth in learning, and Mr. Robert Lenthall, while he continues to teach school, is to have the benefit thereof." —Callender, *Hist. Disc.*, 116. "This," says the Hon. William P. Sheffield, in the *Providence Journal*, 1877, "was the first public school, and Robert Lenthall was the first master of a public school in America." "Although Harvard College was founded in 1638, to provide a learned ministry for the churches, public schools, controlled and maintained by the government for the public good, were not attempted by the Massachusetts Colony until 1647, *Mass. Col. Rec.*, II., 203, nor by the Plymouth Colony until 1672, *Ply. Col. Rec.*, V., 107. See also Baylies' *Memoirs of Ply. Col.*, pt. II, 93. Yet Governor Bradford early conceived the idea of giving instruction to the young of his Colony, but encountered insuperable difficulties."—*Hist. Ply. Plantation;* 4 *Mass. Hist. Coll.*, III., 161; cf. Bacon's *Genesis of the N. E. Chh.*, p. 397; Barrows' *Devel. Bap. Princ. in R. I.*, p.; 89 cf, Arnold, *Hist.*, I., 145. Schools earlier than 1647 had existed in Massachusetts; but they were either connected with the church as parochial schools or maintained by private subscriptions, whose advantages however were offered to the public probably gratuitously, and in this sense only "free"—*Mem. Hist. Bost.*, I., 123; *Mass. Col. Rec.*, II, 6, 9. Thomas Leverett, elder of the First Church, Boston, wrote April 13, 1635: "Likewise it was then generally agreed upon that our brother Philemon Pormost shall be entreated to become schoolmaster for the teaching and nourtering of children with us."—*Mem. Hist. Bost.*, I., 123. Mr. Charles K. Dillaway adds: "This being the only public school for about half a century, it is reasonable to infer that the elementary as well as the higher branches were taught. Its principal object, however, from its establishment to the present time has been to prepare young

This day was rainy, I preached, Mr. Wightman [being] absent.

Fryd., 15. Visited Mrs. Tillinghast being as 'twas conceived near ye point of death, but God raised her, and displayed his glorious power. This night, Mr. Joseph Park, my ancient acquaintance lodged at my house.

Lord's D., 17. Preached in my course, Mrs. Shrief propounded for Baptism. Mrs. Hunt sent for me being sick. Prayed with her.

Mond., 18. Prayed with Mr. James Grinman [Greenman].

Thirsd., 21. Mrs. Eliz^th Shrief Baptized. Exceeding windy weather.

Fryd., 22. The Quakers' addition to their meeting house [136] raised. My family ill.

Lord's D., 24. Mr. Shrief propounded for Baptism. Mr. Claggett's child's funeral bid to.

Tuesd., 26. Prayed with Benjamin Hambey. Very sick. Note from ye life of Mr. Thomas Hooker. He used to say that ye promises of God were as boats to carry perishing sinners over to ye Lord Jesus Christ.

Mond., Septem. 1 Heard Mr. Maxwell intended not to preach any more. This day Mary Ailsworth died. She was sprinkled 4 or 5 days before. W^t Mr. Maxwell said to her encouraged her in it, for she was otherwise inclined.

The fort [137] here began to be rebuilt in ye year 1724, and was finished in ye year 1729.

Tuesd., 2. This day at evening I prayed wth sister Hannah Wilson, whose husband, Mr. Jonathan Wilson, died about 4 of ye clock.

---

men for college." *Ibid*, IV., 237. It is perhaps needless further to add that Mr. Dillaway refers in his words to the justly famous Boston Latin School.

[136] (Wanting.)

[137] *King's Fort* was inadequate to defend the harbor. Queen Ann's Fort was built 1702 on Goat Island, on the site of Fort Woolcot. (*Arnold*, II., 5.) Tax laid 1706 to finish Fort Ann, war having begun. Peace came in 1714 and its garrison was discharged. 1721 Fort Ann was repaired, a loan was made for that purpose. (*Ibid*, II., 25, 54, 69.) In 1727, an address to King George stated " that a regular and beautiful fortification of stone, with a battery had been built at Newport." (*Ibid*, 93.) In 1733, Fort George was armed. (*Ibid, passim*.) Callender, in his Historical Discourse, says: "The necessary defense of the inhabitants was never neglected in time of war, and since the peace, the colony, tho' so small as it is, hath rebuilt an handsome fort on an island that commands the harbor of Newport, and in 1733 furnished it with a number of fine guns at their own expense." In 1775, Fort George was abandoned—a signal established at Tower Hill ; a signal for Tonomy Hill, 1776. In 1776, a new fort was built at the Point in Newport, another on Brenton's Point, and Fort George reconstructed. In 1784, the fort on Goat Island, after bearing successive names of the English sovereigns—Ann and George—was called Washington. (*Arnold*, 511.)

78   THE DIARY OF JOHN COMER.

Wednesd., 3.   This day I prayed with James Grinman, near ye point of expiration. This day also Mr. Rosom's eldest daughter died. This evening I prayed with sister H. Wilson.

At ye sessions in June past ye Assembly past an act for ye Colony to be divided into Counties, viz., Newport County, Providence County, and Kings County, 3 in number.[138]

Note. By a letter to me from Boston, dated Aug. 5th, 1729, I have this information, y^t every night by order from ye Govr, a company in a night, watches; and he intimates y^t he intends it shall be so thro ye winter. The reason of such a watch is because in ye last week in July a mob rose to prevent ye landing of Irish, and to hinder the merchants from sending away ye corn as they attempted.

This day Mr. Bryant's wife died. My aunt Mason came.

Fryd., 5.   This day Mr. Charles Bardine died.

Sat., 6.   This morning I went over to ye Yearly Meeting[139] at North Kingstown, ye wind exceeding high, but blessed be God I got safe over. This day Mr. Everitt began with prayer; 1 began in preaching from y^t word Luk. 24:32; [Mr.] Herindine [Herenden] concluded wth prayer. After sermon Mrs. Eliz^th Moot, of Canterbury, in Connecticut, proposed herself for Baptism. She gave good satisfaction concerning ye work of God upon her soul. 'Twas concluded she should be now baptized, and I was chosen to Baptize her, which was done accordingly; and Mr. Valentine Wightman imposed hands. Lodged at Deacon Pardon Tillinghast's.[140]

Lord's D., 7.   This day Mr. Samuel Maxwell left off preaching. This day 'twas concluded upon, y^t Mr. John Walton[141] should pray and begin in preaching, w^h he did from Rev.

---

[138] See *R. I. Col. Rec.*, IV., 427. Arnold *Hist.*, II, 12, 97. As early as 1704, the colony was divided into two counties, the one embracing the islands and called Rhode Island, the other the mainland, and called Providence Plantations, Newport and Providence being the shire towns respectively. At this second division mentioned by Comer, the first county remained as before, receiving only a new name; the other county was divided into two equal parts, the northern portion being called Providence, the southern, embracing King's Province, receiving the name of Kings County.

[139] This seems to have been a "Quarterly" meeting of the Association of Six Principle Baptists.

[140] Probably the one mentioned by Savage, as a son of the Rev. Pardon Tillinghast, who was born in Providence and removed to East Greenwich.—*Geneal. Dict.*

[141] John Walton was a man of "liberal education," "a practicing physician," who in 1730 was invited to preach in Providence, "where a like reformation might be hoped for," as was then in progress in Newport. Of his views respecting the imposition of hands upon

3 : 20 ; y^t Valentine Wightman should second, w^h he did from Psalms 37 : 27 ; and y^t I should close in preaching, w^h I did from Rom. 5 : 6 ; and y^t Elder Saml Fisk should finish ye meeting wth prayer, which he did. Elder Richard Sweet administered ye sacrament. Mrs. E. Moot communed with ye church.

After ye administration a desire y^t a petition from ye whole body of ye Association might be presented to ye Genl Assembly of Connecticut y^t ye Baptists under y^t Government might be cleared from paying taxes to any ministry but their own,[142] which was put to vote, and by a hand vote it was voted in ye affirmative and y^t day signed by a number in ye name and by order of ye whole Association. A comfortable meeting.

Mond., 8. This day about noon I returned home. Got safely home. I praise God. This morning Brother James Grinman [Greenman] died. This day I prayed with Mrs. Charity Carpenter, being sick.

Tuesd., 9. This day news came to town of Govr Burnet's death, who died on Lord's Day ye 7th instant. Brother Grinman buried. Brother John Walton preached at ye funeral, from Matt. 25 : 10. This day I prayed with Widow James. She is a woman of extraordinary experience.

Here follows an exact coppie of ye petition sent to ye Honourable Genl Assembly of Connecticut, as voted in and by the Association of ye Baptist churches at North Kingston.

To the Honourable Genl Assembly of ye Colony of Connecticut, to be convened at New Haven on ye second Thursday of October next. The humble Memorial of ye Genl Association of ye Baptist churches, convened at North Kingston, on ye 6th day of September, A. D. 1729, humbly showeth, That y^r Honours' Petitioners having sundry Brethren of their Communion dwelling up and down in your Colony, they therefore do hereby humbly crave y^t an Act of Assembly may be passed to free them from paying any taxes to any ministry except their own, and from building any meeting houses except for their own use, humbly hoping your Honours will consider they are utterly unable to maintain their own way of

---

all believers we learn from a letter addressed by Gov. Jenks to the Rev. James Brown, in which he says : " As to what Mr. Walton holds with respect to laying on of hands upon believers as such, I do not understand by him that he opposes it any other ways, than if it be performed for the obtaining the extraordinary gifts of the Holy Ghost ; but he thinks it ought not to be any bar to communion with those who have been rightly baptized."—Backus, *Hist.*, II., 22.

[142] The laws of Connecticut, as well as of Massachusetts, during the early history of New England, were very stringent against all dissenters from the "established" religion. They fell with especial severity upon Baptists and Quakers, who constituted a large proportion of these dissenters.

worship and to pay taxes also to yᵉ Presbyterians, and yᵗ the gracious act of indulgence together with yᵉ reasonableness of our request will be motive sufficient to move yʳ Honours to grant yᵉ request of yʳ Honours' humble Memorialists. Signed in yᵉ name and by yᵉ order of the sᵈ Association, this 8ᵗʰ day of September, A. D. 1729, by

RICHARD SWEET,
VALENTINE WIGHTMAN
SAMUEL FISK, } Elders.
JOHN COMER,
PARDon TILLINGHAST,
JOHN WIGHTMAN,
JAMES KING.
BENJAMIN HERENDEEN, [Herenden.]
TIMOTHY PECKHAM,

JOSEPH HOLMES,
EBENEZER COOK,
GEORGE GARDNER,
THOMAS DURKE,
EBENEZER GRAVES,
JAMES BATES,
JOHN TILLINGHAST,
JOSEPH SANFORD,
SAMUEL WEIGHT.

Here follows what was thought convenient to be added.

To the Honorable Genˡ Assembly of yᵉ Colony of Connecticut to be convened at New Haven, on yᵉ 2ᵈ Thursday of October next, these lines may signifie yᵗ we yᵉ subscribers do heartily concur with yᵉ Memorial of our Brethren on yᵉ other side and humbly request yᵉ same may be granted, which we think will much tend to Christian unity and be serviceable to true religion, and will very much rejoice your Honours' friends and very humble servants.

JOSEPH JENKS, Governour,
JAMES CLARKE, } Elders,
DANIEL WIGHTMAN,
JOHN ODLIN,
EZEKIEL BURROUGHS.

Dated at Newport, September yᵉ 10ᵗʰ, 1729.

There was drawn from yᵉ Treasury of yᵉ Church at Newport, 40s. towards defraying yᵉ Charges in preferring yᵉ Petition.

Wednesd., 10. This day yᵉ lecture was observed instead of Thursday upon yᵉ account of Mr. Walton's being in town to preach. He preached from Matt. 16: 26, what is a man profited if he gain yᵉ whole world, &c.

Thirsd., 11. This day I went to Bristol, with my Aunt Mason, who was bound to Boston. Returned well. I praise yᵉ name of yᵉ Lord. This day Samˡ Hallet and David Richards were cleared by yᵉ jury, who went out twice on yᵉ case.

Fryd., 12. Here I think to note yᵉ letter from yᵉ Association of yᵉ Baptist churches, met at Newport, June 21, 1729, to the brethren belonging to yᵉ meeting house at South Kingstown.

The Association of yᵉ Baptist Churches of our Lord Jesus Christ, sitting at Newport on Rhode Island this 23ᵈ day of June 1729,[143] consisting of the Pastors, Deacons, and Brethren of yᵉ respective churches,

Sendeth Greeting: To the Brethren belonging to yᵉ meeting house in South Kingstown, wishing grace, mercy, and peace, from God our Father and yᵉ Lord Jesus Christ.

We yᵉ above Convention finding ourselves under yᵉ strongest obligation to wish well to yᵉ parts of yᵉ mystical body of Christ in genˡ, and to yᵉ several churches to which we stand more immediately related in particular, and are willing to contribute everything yᵗ lies in our power to yᵗ end, and having been informed of certain difficulties to which you have been exposed and are still; do therefore take yᵉ liberty to write this Christian letter to you, wherein we can't but desire, request, and even exhort you to strive to put yourselves with all convenient speed into yᵉ most exact order yᵗ yᵉ purity of yᵉ gospel requires, and in order thereunto to proceed to choose and set apart some person whom you shall think suitably qualified for yᵉ work of yᵉ ministry, and who upon probation may be solemnly ordained to yᵉ sacred office according to yᵉ tenour of God's word; and upon this occasion, we can't but recommend to you (if you think well of it) our beloved Brother, Daniel Everit, whom God in his Providence hath sent among you, and whose endeavours we hope he hath already blessed for yᵉ good of many souls. And we can't see yᵗ, because his wife is not at this time in communion wᵗʰ you, it is a sufficient bar to obstruct the choice of him.

And we pray yᵗ no self interest may divert you from encouraging him. Upon yᵉ whole, dear Brethren, we commit you to God and to yᵉ word of his grace, humbly praying the God of all grace to make all grace to abound towards you. Wishing you all yᵉ blessings we can wish for our own souls, so committing and commending to yᵉ conduct of Heaven and to yᵉ blessing of yᵗ God who is able to endow you wᵗʰ all good, to whom be glory in all yᵉ churches world without end. Amen.

Newport on Rhode Island, signed in yᵉ name and behalf of yᵉ Association by

DANIEL WIGHTMAN,
VALENTINE WIGHTMAN,
NICHOLAS EYRES, } Elders.
STEPHEN GORTON,
JOHN ODLIN,
JAMES BROWN.

An exact coppie, Newport, June 23ᵈ, 1729.

Saturd., 13. This day Mr. Peleg Carr's wife died. Heard Mr. Crandal from Rev. 19 : 8. Clear gospel sermon.

Lord's D., 14. A child's funeral bid to. Mr. [Mrs.?] Carr buried from yᵉ meeting house. Mr. Maxwell carried on meeting again by reading 4 chapters and praying.

---

[143] This was the meeting mentioned on page 66, Seq.

Mond., 15.　　This day I transcribe from my notes Lord's Day August ye 13th, 1727 what I delivered in a funeral sermon from Ecc. 9 : 5 upon ye death of my wife's father, Mr. John Rogers, being ye sum of his just character, who died suddenly ye Friday morning.

" Hath not ye sudden and surprising death of an exemplary Christian something worthy of some notice and remark? Modesty almost obliged me to pass such a death by, and not to mention it in a Publick Auditory. But duty and gratitude to ye deceased, whose memory is blessed, and benefit to you, strongly and irresistibly engaged me to take notice of a few of ye many Christian virtues which shone wth a very peculiar lustre, thro ye series of almost 59 years. His studiousness and diligence, his watchfulness and integrity in all his undertakings, if we should consider him in all relations, we should find ye spirit of a Christian acting of [in] him. His earnest zeal in ye promotion of Religion, his constant attendance on ye publick ministry of ye word, and his wonderful deportment at ye Table of ye Lord, his seriousness, gravity, and solemnity, are highly worthy of our remark and observation, together with ye many hours of secret communion between God and his own soul, and ye savoury discourses of a work of grace in w^h he took a great delight, give abundant proof y^t he converst in Heaven, while he tabernacled here upon earth.

"Among ye various entertainments of a soul sensibly overcome wth divine love, he took peculiar pleasure and satisfaction in ye doctrines of grace, and in ye illustration of ye excellencies of Christ and ye wonderful Redemption wrought out alone by him, and was willing to ascribe all unto ye riches of Sovereign grace without any merit of his own. He adored Christ as his Lord and trusted in his righteousness as ye great Mediator. He was zealous to maintain ye doctrine of free grace against all opposition whatever.

" His practice and conversation were agreeable to his Christian principles, for he knew y^t ye grace y^t brings salvation teaches a denial of all ungodliness and worldly lust. He was regulated by [the] standing rule of God's word (w^h he took for his guide) thro ye help of ye Holy Spirit at all times. And tho much of his piety was undiscovered from ye mean conception he had of himself, yet so much was apparently made manifest as demonstrated him a real Christian,

" When it pleased God in ye all wise course of his holy providence to invite him into ye glory of his Lord, and to bid a final farewell to all things here below and to take up his abode wth the spirits of just men made perfect.

"The messenger of death in all probable conjecture alarmed all his powers at ye first stroke, which from ye want of natural heat and ye stagnation of ye whole mass of blood, all allowable means were rendered ineffectual. Tho it pleased God to continue to him the use of his senses till the last expiring hours of his life, yet for ends best known to himself by the depriving him almost of his speech and strength he was hindered from handing forth those serious and dying advices he might probably have given. Apprehending in himself ye shortness of his time here, he requested your unworthy minister to recommend him into the hands of God by prayer, and at y^t time he expressed his entire and alone dependence for acceptance wth God to be from the undertakings and merits of the Lord Jesus Christ, and desired a will bowed more and more into ye will of God. Tho he acknowledged himself something straightened, yet with hands and eyes lifted to heaven he said, *The Lord is able to enlarge me.* After a short discourse of ye crown of righteousness which ye Lord ye Righteous Judge will give to [them] y^t love him, being asked whether he expected y^t crown, he replied, *Yes, thro grace; yes, thro grace,* which was ye last entire sentence he uttered for ye consolation of survivors. And in about ye revolution of 24 hours from ye first extreme stroke he fell asleep in ye arms of Jesus, as though he was taking his natural repose, and so [like] holy Simeon he had Christ in his arms—and departed in peace (no doubt) to see the salvation of God. Blessed are ye dead y^t die in ye Lord. Rev. 14 : 13."

Tuesd., 16. This night died Mr. Tuck, a man who came a little before from Boston. He fell off his horse about two miles out of town ye Tuesday before and broke his skull, and received his death wound. 'Tis said he was y^n in drink. He died senseless.

Thirsd., 18. This day I was at Dartmouth at Mr. Philip Tabor's. Preached there from Jno 12 : 21. About 60 auditors. Got home y^t night well. J. W. married. Found all well. I praise God.

Fryd., 19. Visited my people.

Sat., 20. Heard Mr. Crandall from 1 Pet. 1 : 5. Well opened.

Lord's D., 21. Preached in course.

Mond., 22. Visited Brother Jno Proctor and Thomas Butcher whom ye day before came from ye Jersies. At night

B. Proctor came to visit me. This evening I received a letter from Mr. Thomas Symmons,[144] pastor of ye Baptist church in South Carolina.

Tuesd., 23.   This day Mr. Wightman and I went down to ye beach to see ye sein drawn; and did so. I obtained a coppie of a divorce of Sarah Brown, of Providence, from her husband, Jonathan Brown, signed by Mr. Richard Ward, Recorder.

Wednesd., 24.   Visited.

Thirsd., 25.   This day I being sent for to ye Almshouse by Mrs. Steadman being y^n sick; went and prayed with her. She seemed in great terror about her soul. She expressed great fear of death. O, said she with great anguish, I am afraid to die, I am afraid. O may I have my work well done.

Fryd., 26   This day I went to prison to visit Mr. O'Harra, ye Church minister of Providence, being under close confinement 8 days, and a prisoner 21 days, but he was at large and so made his escape, and for y^t reason was closely confined. A doleful place. Lord, I pray thee grant me thy grace and leave me not to commit any ill, so as to expose me to ye difficulties of a prison.

>   A prison is a house of care,
>   A grave for men alive,
>   A tombstone for to try a friend,
>   No place for men to thrive.

Saturd., 27.   This day I received a letter from ye Baptist church in North Carolina,[145] settled about two

---

[144] "Of the early settlers of South Carolina, a considerable proportion were Baptists. They came in separate colonies, about the year 1683, partly from the west of England, and partly from Piscataway in the District of Maine."—Benedict, *Hist.*, II, 120. A church was formed at Charleston, with William Screven as pastor. "In 1699 they erected a brick meeting house," and parsonage house.—*Ibid*. It was of this church that Thomas Simmons was pastor, succeeding the Rev. William Peart. During Mr. Simmon's pastorate, "the church passed through a series of trials, occasioned by the schism and encroachments of the General Baptists." He was the author of a work entitled "Some Queries concerning the Operations of the Holy Spirit Answered," and died January 31, 1747, being succeeded in the pastorate by the Rev. Oliver Hart. [The removal of Baptists from Kittery, Maine, to South Carolina, in 1682 or 1683, according to Dr. Basil Manly, "seems only to have been a transfer of the seat of worship of the persecuted flock (or a majority of it) which had been gathered on the Piscataqua." The church was located first at Somerton, S. C., and removed to Charleston about 1693.—J. W. W.]

[145] "Moore, in his *History of North Carolina*, says, 'Sir William Berkeley, Governor of Virginia, drove out of that Colony, in 1653, the Baptists and Quakers, who found a refuge in the Albemarle region of Carolina.'" "The first church, however, of which we read, was not organized till 1727, in the county of Camden."—*Bap. Ency.* According to Comer, *Diary*, p. 73, it was in the county of Chowan.

years (in yᵉ year 1727) since, by Mr. Paul Palmer,¹⁴⁶ signed by

JOHN PARKER,	THOMAS DARKER,
JOHN JORDAN,	JAMES COPLAND,
BENJAMIN EVANS,	JOHN WELCH,
JOHN PARKER,	JOSEPH PARKE,
JOHN BRINKLEY,	WILLIAM COPLAND,
MICHAEL BRINKLEY,	JOSEPH PARKER.

This church consists of 32 members, it meets at Chowan.

I received a letter on Monday last from [the] South Carolina church. There has been a difficulty in that church with yᵉ minister, Mr. Palmer, but 'tis made up. (As to yᵉ difficulty, it appears by a letter sent to Boston Church, dated April 13, 1728.)

Lord's D., 28. Preached in stated course.

Mond., 29. Mr. Wightman and I went up to visit Mr. Joseph Card, yᵉ aged. He reproved me exceedingly about my wig. I don't know yᵗ I pride myself in it.

Tuesd., 30. This day [I] transcribed yᵉ first Covenant of this Colony and its original, which I had obtained out of yᵉ Records of yᵉ Colony thro yᵉ favour of yᵉ Secretary, Mr. Richard Ward.¹⁴⁷

The Island Aquetneck was purchased of 3 Indian Sachems, viz.,¹⁴⁸ Canonicus, Miantinomi, Wanamitonoment, by Mr. Wil-

---

[146] Paul Palmer was a native of Welsh Tract, Del., where he was baptized by the Rev. Owens Thomas, pastor of the church at that place; removed to North Carolina, where he organized a church, "with which he continued, not, however, without some difficulties, until his death."—Benedict, *Hist.*, II., 97.

[147] Richard Ward was born in Newport April 15, 1689; his father Thomas, and grandfather John, were both members of Cromwell's army, the latter as an officer in the cavalry; both emigrated to this country and settled in Newport, the son about 1660, and the father somewhat later. Richard Ward was Secretary of the Colony for nineteen years, 1714–33; in 1740, was elected Deputy Governor, and upon the death of Governor Wanton, in 1641, became Chief Magistrate; was elected Governor the two following years, 1741–43; and died August 21, 1763. He married Mary, daughter of John Tillinghast, by whom he had fourteen children; one of whom was Samuel, famous for his connection with the "Ward and Hopkins controversy"; another son, Henry, was Secretary of State for thirty-seven years, 1760–97.—E. R. Potter, *Early Hist. Narr.*, 310; *Biog. Cyclop. R. I.*

[148] "West of Pokanoket Country, embracing the islands in and around Narragansett bay, the eastern end of Long Island, with nearly the whole mainland as far as Pawcatuck river, was the powerful tribe of Narragansetts, including several subordinate tribes, all owning the sway of the sagacious and venerable Canonicus, with his brave and generous nephew, Miantonomo, as their chief Sachems."—Arnold, *Hist.*, I., 23. The deed of the Indians conveying lands to the new settlers opens on this wise: "The 24ᵗʰ of yᵉ 1ˢᵗ month called March, in yᵉ yeare (soe commonly called) 1637: Memorandum, That we Cannonicus and Miantunnomu yᵉ two chief Sachims of the Nanhiqqausetts, by virtue of our generall command

liam Coddington and his united friends, for 40 fathoms of white beads, March 24th, 1637-8.

They incorporated into a Body Politick March ye 7th, 1638. This was ye form of ye incorporation: [149]

RHODE ISLAND, March ye 7th, 1638.

We whose names are underwritten dɔ sware solemnly in ye presence of Jehovah to incorporate ourselves into a Body Politick; and [as] he shall help us will submit our persons, lives, and estates, unto our Lord Jesus Christ, the King of kings and Lord of lords, and to all those most perfect and absolute laws of his given us in his holy Word of truth, to be guided and judged thereby.[150]

WILLIAM CODDINGTON,[151]	JOHN CLARKE,[152]
WILLIAM HUTCHINSON,[153]	JOHN COGGESHALL,[154]
WILLIAM ASPINWALL,[155]	SAMUEL WILBOR,[156]
JOHN PORTER,[157]	JOHN SANFORD,[158]
EDWARD HUTCHINSON,[159]	THOMAS SAVAGE,[160]
WILLIAM DYRE,[161]	WILLIAM FREEBORN,[162]
PHILIP SHERMAN,[163]	JOHN WALKER,[164]
RICHARD CARDER,[165]	WILLIAM BOLSTINE,[166]
HENRY BULL,[167]	RANDOL HOLDEN.[168]

of the Bay, as also the particular subjectinge of the dead Sachims of Acquidnecke and Kitackamuckqutt," etc.—*R. I. Col. Rec.*, I., 45. The third sachem mentioned seems to have been subordinate, and resident Sachem of Aquidneck. "This witnesseth that I, Wanamatrannemit [as the name is spelled in the instrument] y^e at present Sachem, inhabitant of ye Island," etc.—*Ibid.*, 47.

[149] The language of this instrument as given by Comer, above, is slightly inaccurate; instead of "do swear . . . to incorporate," it should read, "do here . . . incorporate"; also, instead of "most perfect and absolute laws," it should read, "perfect and most absolute laws."

The Scripture passages given in the original, Comer has omitted; these are Exod. 24 : 3; 2 Chron. 11 : 3, 4; 2 Kings 11 : 17; in regard to which see *Bap. Quart.*, X., 190.

Arnold, *Hist.*, I., 124, assumes that this civil compact was signed at Providence. Prof. J. C. C. Clarke, *Bap. Quart.*, X., 190, claims that it was signed in Boston, adding: "The common assertion that this act was performed in Providence is indefensible."

The signers themselves of this document, Savage, in his *Geneal. Dict.*, describes as "among the best men of Boston."

The authorship of this compact—"the real first charter of Rhode Island"—with the two accompanying "engagements," is unknown. Prof. Clarke thinks "The probabilities of Mr. Clarke's authorship of the documents are conspicuous."

[150] The intensely religious spirit pervading the compact of incorporation has led to a misunderstanding of its purpose. While separating Church from State, the colonists recognized God as the author of both, and in each as the supreme source of authority. "In order to disarm as far as possible all adverse criticism by rival and hostile colonies, and to assure themselves and all future comers, that the State, though denied jurisdiction in the spiritual realm, was nevertheless clothed with divine sanctions, they declared that God was the source of civil authority, and his revealed will, so far as it pertains to the conduct of man with man, should be the fundamental law to govern in civil relations. Thus, while denying to it ecclesiastical rule, they claimed for the State authority delegated by God and recognized by his word."—[Barrows], *Develop. Bap. Principles in R. I.*,

Remark. This day my little daughter was burnt by a coal flying near her eye, but thro God's goodness not in it. O holy

p. 23. Mr. Arnold, *Hist.*, I., 125, 126, who correctly regards this instrument as a "civil compact," and not as "a church covenant," or "a church covenant which also embodied a civil compact," is himself in error when he represents the Aquidneck settlers as limiting their principles of toleration to men professing Christianity, and not making room for those of every faith.—*Bap. Quart.*, VI., 488; X., 191 note; Cf. *Newp. Hist. Magazine*, I., 119–121.

For further discussion of the aims and purposes of these men who settled Rhode Island, see *Origin of the Institutions of Rhode Island*, by the Rev. Samuel Adlam (1871), also *Settlers of Aquidneck and Liberty of Conscience*, by Henry E. Turner, M. D. (1880).

[151] William Coddington was born in 1600; came from Lincolnshire, England, to this country in company with John Winthrop, arriving at Salem, June 12, 1630; was immediately promoted to offices of trust in the Massachusetts Colony; built the first brick house in Boston; in the controversy of 1636–37 he sympathized with the Antinomian party, as did Sir Henry Vane and the Rev. John Cotton; having as a magistrate vainly opposed the violent measures of the government against himself and fellow-adherents of these views, he broke up his extensive mercantile business, and was one of the refugees who found an asylum in Rhode Island. He was prominent in the movement begun in the closing months of 1637, to send out a new colony composed of men who had for their religious opinions fallen under the censures of the Massachusetts authorities. Being a man of wealth and social influence, and having held high office at the Bay, he was made the chief executive in the organization of the infant Commonwealth. Becoming dissatisfied with the complexion of public affairs under the alliance of 1647, he went to England, and succeeded in detaching Rhode Island from the Mainland, and in being commissioned Governor of the former for life. This commission was revoked in 1652. Mr. Coddington subsequently regained in large measure the public confidence; three different times he held the office of President of the Colony. Having embraced the religious views of the Quakers, he was much disturbed by the rough treatment accorded his fellow religionists in Massachusetts and, August 12, 1672, wrote to Governor Bellingham a letter of admonition. Mr. Coddington died November 1, 1678, and was buried ———. To his grandson, William, John Callender dedicated his "invaluable Century Sermon."—Savage, *Geneal. Dict.*

[152] *See* note 131. John Clarke reached Boston in November, 1637, when the town was in a fever of excitement, the Antinomian controversy having reached its culmination. He had had no share in the troubles that had divided the people; but he was not slow in making his election between the two parties, the oppressed and the oppressors, and he was with more than seventy others almost immediately disarmed. He became the counsellor and leader of the men who were being distressed for their consciences. He proposed to them a solution of the difficulties. In his narrative he says: "I was no sooner on shore but there appeared to me differences among them touching the Covenants, and in point of evidencing a man's good estate; some prest hard for the Covenant of works, and for sanctification to be the first and chief evidence; others prest as hard for the Covenant of grace that was established upon better promises, and for the evidence of the Spirit . . . Whereupon I moved the latter, forasmuch as the land was before us and wide enough . . . and for peace sake, to turn aside to the right hand or to the left. The motion was readily accepted, and I was requested, with some others, to seek out a place."—4 *Mass. Hist. Coll.*, II., 23, 24. In studying the records of those early times we are impressed with the fact that, while not holding so prominent offices as some others, he was "the power behind the throne"; that his, more truly than any other, was the guiding mind in the infant commonwealth. From the outset until his death he was busy with public affairs. In 1651, he was sent by a large constituency to England to secure the revocation of Coddington's commission; this task successfully accomplished, he remained in London to watch over the imperilled interests of the colony, and, notwithstanding the opposition of powerful rivals,

Providence. Prayed with Mrs. Charity Carpenter, being very sick.

obtained a charter guaranteeing " privileges unparalleled in the history of the world"; that declared "that no person within the said colony, anytime hereafter, shall be anywise molested, punished, disquieted, or called in question for any differences of opinion on matters of religion." Returning home in 1664, Mr. Clarke's counsels and services were in constant requisition. His last public act was performed only a few days before his death, in making good the defenses of his colony against the savage attacks of the Indians. He died very suddenly, April 20, 1676, while the war of "King Philip" was in progress, menacing the peace and safety of the community. He was buried upon his own land, upon what was afterwards known as Tanner Street (now West Broadway).—Savage, *Gen. Dict.*; Cathcart, *Bap. Ency.*

[John Clarke was a broad-minded, level-headed, strong man; a man of God. In his doctrinal and practical views he was remarkably in accord with Regular Baptists of the present time in this country. He was free from the eccentricities which appeared in the life of the celebrated Roger Williams. More than any other man he is entitled to be called the Founder of the Baptist Denomination in America. His large participation in the public and political affairs of the infant colony was rendered necessary by imperative circumstances, and can be abundantly justified without regarding it as a precedent for political activity on the part of ministers in an old and settled community. His fame has not equaled his merits, but it is to be hoped that future historians will do him fuller justice. I know that in this estimate of John Clarke I voice the opinion of the author of these Notes.—J. W. W.]

[153] William Hutchinson was born in Lincolnshire, England, about —— reached Boston, September 18, 1634, where he became a member of the First Church on the 16th of October, and a freeman the following 4th of March. He is described as a merchant, and as being possessed of "a good estate." It was his wife, Anne, who became so conspicuous in Boston in connection with the Antinomian controversy, and upon whom the severity of Massachusetts law fell so heavily. Banished from Massachusetts, the wife was not deserted by her husband; he took his family to Rhode Island. He held the office of treasurer of the Colony, and when the division took place, and most of the public officers removed to the south and settled Newport, he was made chief executive of those remaining at Portsmouth, the original settlement. He died 1642. The year after his death, his wife removed to the Dutch Province, and before she was fairly established was murdered by the Indians. Mrs. Hutchinson was in many respects a remarkable woman, and must have been richly endowed; but it is a mistake to make her a prominent figure in the early history of the new colony; to represent her as in any sense a leader in the movement to settle Rhode Island; indeed, it does not appear that she had any share even in the counsels that led to that result. Their daughter Faith married Thomas Savage.

[154] John Coggeshall came from Essex, England, arriving at —— September 16, 1632; admitted a freeman the 6th of November following; removed to Boston; was a representative in the General Court for several years; sympathizing with the Antinomians he was expelled from his seat, disarmed, and banished; went to Rhode Island, chosen Assistant, then President of the Colony. After filling other honorable positions, he died, probably in November, 1689. His son, John, married Elizabeth, youngest daughter of William Baulston.

[155] William Aspinwall came to this country in 1630, probably in the fleet bringing John Winthrop; was one of the earliest members of the church in Charlestown, and chosen one of the two deacons; soon removed to Boston, became a freeman April 3, 1632, and in 1637 a representative in the General Court; sympathizing with the Antinomian party in 1637, he was "dismissed, disarmed, disfranchised, and banished"; entered "with so many other of his fellow-saints" the movement to found a new Colony in Rhode Island in 1638, and at its organization he became the secretary. But his connection with the Colony was

| Wednesd., October 1. | This day I received a letter from ye prison from Mr. O'Hara. |

not of long duration, for he went to New Haven in 1641, where he lived a couple of years, and thence returned to Boston.—Savage, *Geneal. Dict.*

156 Samuel Wilbor came to Boston before 1633, where he resided in 1637, and "fell into sympathy with the major part of his fellow-worshippers under the dangerous doctrines of Cotton and Wheelwright, so that the body of the people at other places in the Colony deemed it necessary to disarm them in November, 1637"; with eighteen others, "among the best men of Boston," he assisted to purchase and settle Aquidneck, or Rhode Island; 'was held in high esteem, so that after his removal to Taunton his name was retained on the list of freemen in 1652. Savage says he had wisdom enough to hold on to his estates at Portsmouth, at Taunton, and at Boston, returning to the latter place before making his will, April 30, 1656. He died on the 29th of the September following. His eldest son, Samuel, married a daughter of John Porter, and was named in the royal charter as one of the patentees. *Ibid.* Sheffield differs from some of these statements.

157 John Porter became a freeman at Roxbury, November 5, 1633, whence he removed to Boston, becoming an adherent of the Antinomian views in 1637, was one of the company removing to Rhode Island in 1638, was an Assistant in the new Colony in 1641, removed to Wickford [or Warwick, as Sheffield states], where he was living in 1674.

158 John Sanford was in Boston in 1631, and member of the church there, admitted freeman April 3, 1632, and same year made cannoneer at the fort; as an Antinomian was in 1637 disarmed; came to Rhode Island with first settlers, where he held many offices of trust, being successively Constable, Treasurer, Secretary, Assistant, and President of the Colony in May, 1653. The time is not known. His eldest son, John, married April 17, 1663, Mary, daughter of Samuel Gorton, and widow of Peter Greene.

159 Edward Hutchinson, eldest son of William, (note 153), called Jr. to distinguish him from his uncle of the same name, to whose name was appended Sen., came a single man to Boston before his parents, and became a member of the church, and freeman September 3, 1634; was among the first settlers of Rhode Island, but in a few years returned to Boston, where he opposed the cruel measures of the government toward the Quakers. He died August 19, 1675, aged 62 years.

160 Thomas Savage, son of William, of Somersetshire, England, came to Boston in 1635, at the age of 27, became a member of the Boston Church, and a freeman May 25, 1635; entered upon the business of a merchant; was disarmed in November, 1637, and removed with eighteen others to Rhode Island, where he remained however but a short time, for becoming reconciled with the Boston authorities he returned to dwell [there]. He married Faith, daughter of William and Anne Hutchinson.

161 William Dyre came from London to Boston in 1635, became a member of the Boston Church, a freeman March 3, 1636, was disarmed and disfranchised in 1637 for his Antinomianism; was of the company removing to Rhode Island in 1638, where he was held in high esteem; he was clerk of the General Court, Secretary of the Colony, and Attorney-General when the office was created in 1650. His wife, Mary, a religious enthusiast, was hanged in Boston, in 1660. One of their sons was named Mahershalalhashbaz; their other children had ordinary names.

162 William Freeborn, who came from Boston to Rhode Island, in 1637, died at Portsmouth, June 3, 1670, aged 80 years.

163 Philip Sherman arrived at Roxbury, in 1633, a single man; became a freeman May 14, 1634; married Sarah Odding, daughter of the wife of John Porter, by a former husband; was a member of the Boston Church, but led away in 1637 to "familism" (Savage), by Porter, as is supposed, and disarmed; removed to Rhode Island with the first colonists, where he was at one time Secretary of the Colony; he died in 1676.

164 John Walker arrived at Roxbury, and became a member of the church, and admitted freeman May 14, 1634; removed to Boston "to find perhaps wider sympathy for his heresy," was disarmed in 1637 "with the major part of his fellow-worshippers"; removed

Fryd., 3.   This day I attended ye funeral of Mr. Joseph Borden from his house to ye Quakers' meeting house; John Wanton,[169] Dep^y Govr preached. He died suddenly on

to Rhode Island with the first settlers in 1638; in the division of the Colony in 1639, he went with the larger number to the south to settle Newport; his name appears on the roll of freemen at Newport, March 16, 1641, for the last time.

[165] Richard Carder first appears at Roxbury, whence he early removed to Boston, became freeman May 25, 1636; "as a supporter of the pestilent heresy" of the Antinomians, was disarmed and disfranchised in 1637; removed to Rhode Island with other colonists in 1638; in 1643 was engaged with Samuel Gorton, Randall Holden, Richard Waterman, and others in the purchase of Warwick; was, in defending his rights, imprisoned at Roxbury, and placed in irons and threatened with death; was however released, and he lived in peace at Warwick until the breaking out of King Philip's war, when he fled to Newport for protection, where he died in 1676. His family afterward returned to Warwick. Susanna Carder, supposed to be a daughter of Richard, married Nathaniel, son of Richard Waterman.

[166] William Baulston, or Balstone, was admitted a freeman at Boston, October 19, 1630, and was in steady employment for the town until 1637, having been "trusted among the worthiest"; was chosen selectman in 1637, but was in the autumn of that year disarmed "with a majority of his fellow-worshippers for Antinomianism"; after his removal to Rhode Island was assistant in 1639, 41, 56; he died March 14, 1679, aged 78.—Savage, *Gen. Dict.*

[167] Henry Bull was born in 1610, arrived at Roxbury in 1635, became a freeman May 17, 1637, removed to Boston, and became infected with the new views gaining such wide currency; the Roxbury Church records say, "being weak and affectionate, was taken and transported with the opinion of familism, etc., as may be seen in that story," referring to the book sent forth by Mr. Welde, the Roxbury pastor, in which he characterizes Anne Hutchinson as a "Jezebel"; falling with others under the displeasure of the government, he removed in 1638 to Rhode Island, where he became the Colony's first Sergeant in 1685, and 1689 was Governor of the Colony; he died January 22, 1693-4, and was buried in the Coddington burying ground, on Farewell street. His first wife was Elizabeth, who died October 1, 1665; his second wife was Anne Clayton, widow of Nicholas Easton, who died June 3, 1707. He built the stone house on Spring street, which is still standing, the only building erected by "the first comers" now remaining.

[168] Randall Holden came from Wiltshire, England; his name does not appear in any record of the New World until found as one of the witnesses to the deed of the Indian Sachems conveying Aquidneck to the first settlers. His name in this list of signers of the compact of incorporation has occasioned scholars some little difficulty. Comer in the above list omits the name of Edward Hutchinson, sen., and gives Randall Holden, making the number eighteen. Callender, *Hist. Disc.*, p. 84, gives Edward Hutchinson, sen., and omits Randall Holden, making the number eighteen, as does Comer. Backus gives the number of signers as nineteen, including both the above names. The *R. I. Col. Rec.*, also give the number of names as nineteen. Arnold, *Hist.*, I., 124, says, "Holden's is separated from the others by a line." "There were eighteen original proprietors and nineteen signers of the compact." Holden could not have been one of the purchasers, as his name appears as one of the witnesses to the deed.

[169] John Wanton, son of Edward and Elizabeth Wanton, was born in 1672; "was deputy governor from 1721 to 1722, and from 1729 to 1734, when, upon the death of his brother William, he was elected Governor seven times successively;" thus for twelve consecutive years, "the first five as deputy governor and the last seven as chief magistrate, he had held the highest offices of the State," when he died while still in office, July 5, 1740, and was buried in the Clifton burying ground on Golden Hill street, in Newport. He was for many years an approved minister of the Society of Friends, and is said to have been very eloquent.—Arnold, *Hist.*, II., 126; *Biog. Cyclop. R. I.*

Wednesday evening before 9 of ye clock. He was abroad on his horse about sunset.

The voice of sudden death is y^t—Be you also ready. O may I be so. From ye Monthly Mercury for June 1729 in London, were christened 1279 and buried 1805; there decreased 716.

Sat., 4. Attended church meeting.

Lord's D., 5. This morning I was sent for to pray with Mr. Daniel Shrief who was exceeding low—Did so—and again at evening.

Mond., 6. Prayed wth Mr. Daniel Shrief.

Tuesd., 7. Visited Mr. Barker and Capt. Peckcom in ye woods.[170] I have not been there before [in] 9 months. This 7th of Octr I paid Capt. Peckcom ye use money for ye fifty pounds he took up for me of ye Colony, w^h was £2 10s. 0d. So y^t there is one bond taken up.

Wednesd., 8. Exceedingly beyond measure almost bowed down and depress^t in my spirits about living in ye O [world?] —circumstances low, and my spirits low even to an extreme, about ye affairs of my former flock. The ark of God is taken—the candlestick is shaking. O y^t ye church, if worthy, may be supplied by Thee, O Lord God. Find and send by him whom Thou wilt send. I am also so low in spirit y^t I can't see the end why ye holy God is contending with me. O Lord show me; lead me in ye way everlasting. I am in much fear about my soul; my precious soul I want to see it precious to God. Lord, I fear I have no oyl [oil]. O, let me know I have oyl [oil] by my lamp burning brighter.

Thirsd., 9. This morning Mr. Crandall and I visited Mr. Shrief. I prayed wth him upon request.

Saturd., 11. Heard Mr. Crandall and Mr. Hiscox from y^t word, He y^t is ashamed of me and of my ways in this sinful—

Lord's D., 12. Mr. Hiscox preached in our congregation from 1 Peter 4 : 18. Well opened. Mr. Henry Loveall preached in ye evening by candle light in ye meeting house.

---

[170] Previous to the Revolution, the island of Rhode Island seems to have been well wooded. The outskirts of the town of Newport were designated "the woods." Thus we read that about 1710 and later, school teachers were elected for the "woods part of the town," while in 1714 one was " chosen school master for the town part of this township"; and that in 1723, an order was passed appropriating from the Public Treasury money for building "the school house in the woods."—*Early School History of Newport*, by Benj. B. Howland, in the *Newport Mercury*, December 4th and 18th, 1875, January 15th and 29th, 1876; *An. Rep. Sch. Com. of Newport*, 1876 or 1877, pp. 53-56.

Mond., 13. Mr. Henry Loveall signified his desire to visit ye churches in the Jersies and earnestly requested a line from ye ministers here. I was desired to draw a few lines. An exact coppie.

These lines may signifie to the Baptized churches of our Lord Jesus Christ in the Jersies and places adjacent, That our Brother, Henry Loveall, the bearer, having had a desire to make a visit into your parts, we do by these signifie to you y^t we know nothing but y^t his conversation is agreeable to ye gospel of Jesus Christ. We would further notifie to you y^t he has been sometimes exercised in ye ministration of ye word. These therefore are to recommend him unto the communion and fellowship of ye churches among you where God in his holy providence may cast him.

So committing both you and him to ye conduct and protection of heaven, earnestly wishing you all ye blessing of ye everlasting covenant, we subscribe ourselves your affectionate Brethren in ye bonds of ye gospel of Jesus Christ our Lord.
JAMES CLARKE,
DANIEL WIGHTMAN.
JOHN COMER.

Newport on Rhode Island, Octr ye 13, 1729.

Here follows w^t I gave him privately:

Brother Loveall: I earnestly wish ye Lord to be with you in your intended journey and desire you would gratifie me in ye following particulars. (1) In each place you go to strive to know in w^t year ye ch was first constituted. (2) W^t number of members they respectively consist of at this time. (3) W^t is their constitution in principles, whether gen^l or particular. (4) W^t are their terms of communion. (5) W^t year ye agreement was made in to hold communion at ye table of the Lord wth such as were not under imposition of hands. (6) How many churches there are in communion. (7) Be sure to present my hearty respects to each church. (8) Endeavor to do all possible good among them y^t you can. These things from your loving B^r, JOHN COMER.

N. Rhode Island, Octr ye 13, 1729.

He had gathered here towards it, £4 15s. 0d.[?]

This evening, in Mr. Thurston's tan vats,[171] a child of Mr. Willm Claggett's [172] was drowned.

---

[171] Wanting.

[172] William Claggett was a clock-maker in Newport, and of considerable celebrity in his day. Several of his tall clocks of elegant workmanship may still be found in the homes of Newport, keeping good time, and serving as ornamental pieces of furniture. He was a man of marked ingenuity, and was possessed of an inquiring mind. The subject of electricity which was then just beginning to attract the attention of scholars, was made by him a profound study. He is said to have anticipated Franklin in some of his experiments. He constructed for his use an electrical machine of large dimensions, which Franklin saw on a visit to Newport. Although the latter "had made some electrical experiments by the friction of glass jars, yet this was the first machine of the kind he had ever seen." This machine is in the possession of the heirs of the late Doctor David King. Mr. Claggett pub-

Tuesd., 14. This day I received a letter from Mr. James Brown, minister at Providence. Here follows w^t he wrote concerning what I wrote to him for to be sent to [the] South Carolina church. An exact coppie.

Providence in ye Colony of Rhode Island in New England, Octr 2, 1727. Jonathan Brown[172½] did confess Christ and was Baptized in his name; for instance David Eldrege was Baptized at ye same time and Jonathan Brown as far as we know walked orderly for some time, but yⁿ grew cold in his religion—Difference arising between him and his wife—and it was reported that he used strong drink to excess; but this not being proved as matter of fact, we did only advise him to better watchfulness and warn him of ye danger to come, which was done several times, but he left his place in ye church, and so left the town. The woman y^t was his wife is yet alive; she was divorced by an act of Court which she obtained after long suit for it.

JAMES BROWN, Pastor,
TIMOTHY SHELDON,
JOHN DEXTER,
JOHN STONE.

Also this day there were 3 funerals in the town, and two persons besides lay dead. The funerals were, Mary Weeden, Willm Claggett's child, and Jonathan Clarke's child. Those who lay dead were Joseph Card aged 81 years, and Mr. Jackson.

Wednesd., 15. This day I completed ye gathering y^t I made in order to send to England to get a set of Mr. Joseph Stennett's works.

	£	s.	d
John Odlin	0	5	0
James Green	0	10	0
Reuben Packcom	0	5	0
Joseph Sanford	0	10	0
Mary Herod	1	0	0
Abigal Dyre	0	10	0
Dinah Packcom	0	5	0
Elizth Fortine	1	0	0
Elizth Tillinghast	0	10	0
Total	4	15	0

lished a tract entitled, *A Looking Glass*, etc., which is very rare, and for a copy of which twenty-five dollars has been refused. He was born in 1696, it is said, in Wales; came to Boston, where he learned the trade of clock-making, probably of Benjamin Bagnall, who was in business in Boston, in 1718; married Mary, daughter of Matthew and Margaret Armstrong, of Boston, who owned an estate in Middle Street, now Hanover Street; was admitted a freeman at Newport May 3, 1726; was a Notary Public in August, 1746; had a second wife, Rebecca, who survived him, and was mentioned in his will; he died in Newport, October 18, 1749, and was buried in the common burying ground.

[172½] See page 84.

Thirsd., 16. Preached at yᵉ place of Baptizing. Joseph Card buried.

Saturd., 18. This day I read over yᵉ affairs of the trouble in yᵉ church to Elder Ephraim Wheaton, who came down to visit my former people. I don't find by him any repentance in yᵐ for ill management, neither do I learn any good desires in yᵐ.

Lord's D., 19. Preached in course. Elder Wheaton administered the Sacrament of yᵉ Lord's Supper to my people. This is yᵉ 2ᵈ time this year.

Mond., 20. Visited my people, and Mr. Clap; he said if people would but weigh yᵉ affair of divine grace in yᵉ scale of right reason expressed to fallen man and not to fallen angels 'twould serve to convince them of yᵉ greatness and sovereignty of it. Divine grace is free to all, but more free to some.

Wednesd., 22. Prayed with Daniel Shrief, continuing low. This day came news of yᵉ small pox being in Boston. It came in about yᵉ middle of yᵉ month, brought in an Irish vessel, who (as I hear) threw over 19 in their passage.

Thirsd., 23. This day instead of a lecture, a funeral sermon was preached by Mr. Wightman in yᵉ meeting house, over yᵉ corpse of Mr. Peleg Carr's little daughter.

Mond., 27. Visited Mr. Clap; in discourse he said that holy things were too good and wicked things too bad, for banter and laughter. True words. Mr. Jno Adams visited me.

Wednesd., 29. My antient acquaintance Mr. John Hobbs visited me.

Thirsd., 30. Exceeding rainy; preached from Luk. 10:42, but 12 people at lecture.

Fryd., 31. Attended Mr. Crandall's meeting. Mrs. Lydia Ryder Baptized by him. A small auditory.

Saturd., Novemr 1. Attended Mr. Crandall's meeting, Mrs. Lydia Ryder passed under hands. This day 4 years I came to live on Rhode Island.

Lord's D., 2. Preached in course. At even Mr. Constant Devotion visited me.

Tuesd., 4. Here I would observe the admirable providence of my good God towards me in his divine preservation shown to me and mine. 'Tis this. On Thursday, May the 15ᵗʰ my mother being in the forenoon about 10 of yᵉ clock in yᵉ chamber bedroom, laid down her pipe in a chair near yᵉ bed and not so well observing whether there were any fire or no, soon went down stairs. A little time after, my wife going up smelt something burn, and going into ye room found it full of smoke and a cap in ye chair ready to blaze, and by y^t means it was extinguished. O w^t a cause have I to bless ye Lord for his protection and goodness. This I penned in a small note which occasioned its being misplaced.

Wednesd., 5. This day I wrote a letter to Mr. Thomas Symmonds, pastor of the Baptist Church in South Carolina. This evening, about seven of ye clock, in the North appeared and continued for several hours a bright light of a large extent like ye breaking of the day. It had a slow motion towards the East, as all ye appearances of y^t like nature have had, tho there were no spears in it as I discovered.

Thirsd., 6. Preached. Mr. Wightman at Narragansett.

Fryd., 7. Wrote a letter to ye church at Chowan, in North Carolina.

Tuesd., 11. This day died Saml Clarke, a youth.

Wednesd., 12. This day I set out on a journey to Swanzey, on foot; got there about four of ye clock to Mr. Callender's chamber. Lodged y^t night at Deacon Kingsley's; much tired. (This day died at N. port Mr. James Noice [Noyes], a young gentleman, educated at Yale Colledge in Connecticut.) The schoolhouse raised.

Thirsd., 13. This being public Thanksgiving through the Province, I preached at Swanzey, in Elder Mason's congregation. Small auditory. Dined with Mr. Callender. Comfortable day. Lodged y^t night with Mr. Jno Callender. (This day died at N. port Major Nathl Sheffield.[173])

Fryd., 14. This day I went over to Providence. Borrowed Mr. Willm Turner's horse. Got there about 3 P. M. Visited Capt. Willm Potter, who was supposed near his end. He knew me but wasn't in a capacity to discourse.

Saturd., 15. This morning about break of day Capt. Potter died, a worthy member of ye Baptist Church in Providence, much lamented. I was requested the next day to

---

[173] Nathaniel Sheffield was the son of Ichabod (of Joseph) and of Mary Parker (daughter of George), and was born April 8, 1667; married Mary ——, who died in 1707, aged 35; married again Katharine Gould, widow of James, and daughter of Walter Clarke, who died January 25, 1752, aged 83, having survived her husband many years. Mr. Sheffield was in public service; was deputy from Newport almost continuously from 1699 to 1713; General Treasurer of the Colony from 1705 to 1707; in 1711 was appointed major of the forces on the Islands; he died November 13, 1729, aged 63.—From *MS.* of W. P. Sheffield, Esq.

preach yᵉ funeral sermon. This day a snow fell deep,—the first. Lodged at Col. N. Powers.

Lord's D., 16. This day I preached at yᵉ funeral of Capt. Potter, at yᵉ meeting house in Providence, from these words, Ps. 116 : 15, Precious in the sight of yᵉ Lord is the death of his saints. A vast auditory of all sorts of people. After prayer, Joseph Smith, a Quaker, said a few words moderately. Lodged at Col. N. Powers'.

Mond., 17. This day twelve months ago the sermon which offended my people was preached. I adore divine goodness expressed towards me in carrying me through yᵗ sinking trouble I met wᵗʰ from yᵐ. Remained at Providence. Lodged at Justice Tillinghast's.

Tuesd., 18. This day visited Elder Brown and Deacon Winsor.[174] My horse sent to Swanzey. This evening I was entertained with a rare water-melon at Col. Powers' yᵗ grew in his garden. Lodged at Justice Tillinghast's.

Wednesd., 19. This day about sunset Mr. Dodge's sloop set sail for N. port, in which I obtained a passage. We arrived at N. port about ten of yᵉ clock yᵗ night. A very comfortable passage. Got safe home. Blessed be yᵉ Lord.

Thirsd., 20. Preached at yᵉ lecture in my wonted course.

Fryd., 21. The letter my people sent to Swanzey for help I saw in yᵉ church book, dated at N. port Sept. 15th. Signed by

        WILLM PECKCOM, Elder,
        SAM'L MAXWELL, Deacon,
        GEORGE HALL,
        JAMES PECKCOM.

Lord's D., 23. This evening after yᵉ service of yᵉ day was over Mr. Hiscox preached in our meet'g house an evening lecture, the 2ᵈ in yᵗ place.

Mond., 24. Visited. This day I record yᵉ comfortable account which I received, that on Thursday the 6ᵗʰ of this month yᵉ Baptist church in Swanzey and yᵉ brethren belonging to Palmer's River, joined together again, after they had stood off near four years, and yᵉ Lord's day following communed together. I desire to praise God for it.

Tuesd., 25. This day I wrote a letter to Deacon Prime of New Milford in Connecticut.

---

[174] (Wanting.)

Thirsd., 27. This day I received a letter from Mr. Callender of Boston and from Deacon Job Shepherd of Cohansey. Preached in stated course.
This day also was found a man drowned at Mr. Goldin's wharf, a sailor, supposed to be drowned y° day before.

Fryd., 28. This day attended Mr. Jn° Adams' lecture; he preached from Matt. 22 : 12.

Saturd., 29. This day I wrote to Mr. Stephen Gorton, of New London. Mr. Job Sanford visited me, being just going to sea.

Lord's D., 30. Preached in course. Prayed with Mr. Benjamin Burroughs between meetings, and at night.

Mond., Decem'r 1. This day wrote a letter to Mr. Palmer, minister at N. Carolina, by Mr. Pierce.

Wednesd., 3. This day I received y° account of y° apparition to Joseph Goodhue.

Fryd., 5. This day I wrote a letter to Nicholas Eyres, minister at New York.

Wednesd., 10. Wrote a letter to Br. E. Callender in Boston. This day the news of Capt. Russell's death came to town. Mr. Jn° Callender came to visit.

Thirsd., 11. Visited Mrs. Russell on y° death of her husband.

Lord's D., 14. Preached in course. Between meetings Mr. Stephen Gorton and I went over to my old meeting house to hear Mr. Callender. 'Tis eleven months since I was in it. This evening I received a letter from Mr. Paul Palmer, minister at N. Carolina. He sent me a small token of love.

Mond., 15. This evening Mr. Gorton preached at R. Gardner's house.

Thirsd., 18. This day Mr. Joshua Clark's funeral was bid to. He died y° night before. Mr. Sam¹ Maxwell at lecture y° 1st time.

Fryd., 19. Attended Mr. Clark's funeral. Visited sundry brethren in y° woods. This day James Clark, a young man, son of Lawrence Clark, died.

Lord's D., 21. Preached in course.

Wednesd., 24. Brother John Proctor paid me a visit.

Thirsd., 25. Mr. Sam¹ Maxwell attended lecture. O y⁴ brotherly love if it be God's will may be renewed and established. I am sure I delight in it.

Attended Mrs. Matthews' funeral who died y° day before.

I

This evening just after nine an alarm was beat to find a little boy y^t was missing who lived wth Henry Saben.

Fryd., 26. This morning Gideon Wanton's [175] child's funeral bid to.

Lord's D., 28. Preached in course. This day the council met about ye small pox.

Wednesd., 31. As to the affairs of the past year, I have met with many things hard and exceedingly uncomfortable, especially about my church in their ill carriage to me; but I have found ye Lord wonderfully supporting of me under it, praised be his holy name.

It has I think been the most trying year to me on many accounts.

There have been this year two drowned; one found dead in his boat, Mr. Updike; one stood in the pillory and [was] clipt.

There have been seventeen received into the church to whom I preach. This year I Baptized one as a minister at large, *i. e.*, under no obligation as pastor to any particular flock, at Narragansett Yearly Association—Elizabeth Moot.

A Presbyterian meeting house built.

What I had this year for support from the church and congregation amounts to £129 0s. 0d.

An exact account of what I owe in the world this first day of January, 1730, John Comer.

	£	s.	d.
To the Colony	50	0	0
" Mr. Jno Odlin	50	0	0
" Sister Eliz^th Barker	40	0	0
" Mother Rogers	40	0	0
" Mr. Arnold Collins	40	0	0
" Mr. Willm Swan	16	0	0
" Mr. John Clarke	5	0	0
" Mr. Jonathan Kingsley	12	0	0
" Madam Judith Cranstone	20	0	0
" Sundries in small debts	18	0	0
Total	291	0	0

[175] Gideon Wanton, son of Joseph and Sarah (Freeborn) Wanton, was born in Tiverton, October 20, 1693; married February 6, 1718, Mrs. Mary Codman, who died September 3, 1780; for two years, 1746–47, held the office of Governor. While in office, responded to the call for troops to assist in carrying on the war against France. The people nobly supported him, but "no man took a deeper interest in it than the Quaker Governor of Rhode Island." Mr. Bartlett says: "That although a Quaker, he was a belligerent one, and fully equal to the emergency, and had he been Governor and Captain-General of Rhode Island in 1861, would have been among the first to send a regiment of Rhode Island volunteers to Washington." He died September 12, 1767.—*Biog. Cyclop., R. I.*

My house in which I now live which was built by me and first inhabited Sept. the 23ᵈ, 1728, cost according to my most exact computation for the bare materials and building together with the land on wʰ it stands £302 3s. 6d. I was lately offered if I would sell it £340, under which if I did sell I could not do it, because I was favored by several in yᵉ price of sundry materials, which, were I now to build, and yᵉ money being so much fallen in its currency, it would cost me so [much] if not more. What I have in the house if priced as to utensils amounts to about £150.

	£	s	d
House	302	3	6
Household utensils	150	0	0
Amounts to	452	3	6
Debts	291	0	0
Remains by subtracting my clear estate	161	3	6

So that I find I have a sufficiency to pay all to whom I owe anything in the world if I should be speedily taken away. I commit my soul unto yᵉ hands of God who gave it me, and my body to be decently interred at yᵉ discretion of my surviving friends, hoping through the merits of Jesus Christ to obtain yᵉ free remission of all my sins and an inheritance among yᵐ yᵗ are sanctified; and [I] bequeath after my just debts are paid yᵉ remainder, £161 3s 6d, unto my dear wife and tender babes, to whom it justly and principally doth belong. So committing them to the Lord who is able fully to supply them, desiring the God of peace that brought again from yᵉ dead yᵉ Lord Jesus Christ, the great Shepherd of yᵉ sheep, might thro' yᵉ blood of the everlasting covenant make them perfect to do his will; working in yᵐ yᵗ wʰ is well pleasing in his sight thro Jesus Christ, to whom be glory, honour, and praise, world without end. Amen.

JOHN COMER.

Newport in Rhode Island,
January the 1st, 1730.

Lord's D., January 1, 1730. This day I begin a new year. Oh that all things may become new within me! Oh that I may purge out yᵉ old leaven yᵗ so I may be a new lump unto the Lord! 1 Cor. 5 : 7.

Fryd., 2. This day Mr. Davis died.

Saturd., 3. Attended Church meeting.

Lord's D., 4.	Preached in course.
Tuesd., 6.	Mrs. Arault's funeral bid to. Mr. John Hobbs visited me.
Wednesd., 14.	My brother James Phillips came to this Island in order to sail hence to y[e] West Indies and London.
Fryd., 23.	This day I wrote a letter to y[e] Baptists at Springfield, directed to Doctor John Leonard.
Lord's D., 25.	This day being sent for I prayed with Mrs. Eady being sick.
Fryd., 30.	This day Mr. Wightman went to y[e] almshouse to visit Hannah Weston. Upon request I prayed with her.
Lord's D., February 1.	This [day] preached in course.
Mond., 2.	This morning a woman named Becks, at y[e] Point, was found dead in her bed. 'Twas supposed she died in her sleep being alone.
Tuesd., 3.	This day I preached at y[e] funeral of Mr. R. Gardner's child.
Wednesd., 4.	This night between nine and ten of y[e] clock in y[e] North appeared the aurora borealis, having many bright streamers extending towards the zenith.
Fryd., 6.	This day Col. William Coddington [176] and Jahleel Brenton [177], two of the Committee for signing y[e] bills of public credit, went to Boston to attend the court, at which were to be tried y[e] next week Paul Eunice, who was found in uttering (and suspected for counterfeiting) sundry bills of this Colony, in Nov[r] past.
Mond., 9.	Prayed with y[e] widow Thurston's child, being very low.
Lord's D., 15.	This day Mr. Maxwell stopt y[e] church and proposed for Mr. John Walton to be sent for to supply my place in y[e] church w[h] was under my care, which was concluded in y[e] affirmative. I learn y[t] Mr. Will[m] Claggett is a principal instrument in y[t] affair. I am informed y[t] Philip Smith is something delirious; y[t] y[e] same wicked spirit still rules in Edward Smith and Capt Will[m] Peckcom as in y[e] height of y[e] difference, who were y[e] principal wicked instruments in it, tho they were willing to lay all upon me, w[h] is utterly false. But I am supported by God's infinite grace and this day by y[t] word, Psalm 37 : 1, 7, 8, 9. Fret not thyself because of evil doers.

---

[176] and [177] (Wanting).

This evening Mr. Jn⁰ Callender was married at Swanzey to Mrs. Elizabeth Hardin.

This day Mr. Jn⁰ Callender preached his farewell sermon at Swanzey from Ps. 133 : 1, and proposed to lay down yᵉ ministry altogether.

The interest of Christ in yᵉ Baptist churches looks very dark at this time; the harvest is great, but yᵉ labourers are few. Oh yᵗ yᵉ Lord of yᵉ harvest would furnish and send forth into his harvest! I mourn over yᵉ churches. Lord show wᵗ is yᵉ ground of thy controversie.

The trouble at Swanzey was on yᵉ account of Mr. Callender, in that some were willing to divert my settling there in yᵉ year 1725, because yᵉ way might be open for him, which was two years before he was a professor. He was baptized in Boston in June 1727, in wʰ month he began his public ministry in Boston, and about yᵉ month of August, 1728, he began to preach at Swanzey and continued to do so till ¦Feb. yᵉ 15, 1730. On yᵉ day yᵉ church met to choose him to office he signified his design to desist yᵉ service, to the great trouble and surprise of the church.

Thirsd., 19. This day died Mrs. Elizᵗʰ Coddington widow of Mr. Edward Coddington.

Wednesd., 25. This day Mr. Adams' church met to give him a dismission from his charge, which was accordingly done, but no letter of recommendation. He came to this Island August 5, 1727. Mr. Adams preached in the schoolhouse January yᵉ 21, 1728; was ordained April yᵉ 11, 1728; was dismisst, February yᵉ 25, 1730; removed out of town March yᵉ 2, 1730; his people had contended with him about a year. Though there be troubles yet God's foundation is sure.

Thirsd., 26. This day prayed with Mrs. Bingham, being sick.

Fryd., 27. This day prayed with her again.

Mond., March 2. This day I went to visit Mr. Jn⁰ Adams, being just going out of town. I received a letter from Mr. Symmonds, minister at South Carolina.

Tuesd., 3. This day I went to visit Elder Peckcom, who discoursed to my satisfaction about yᵉ trouble and yᵉ things of God.

Thirsd., 5. This day Edward Thurston's child was buried from yᵉ meeting house; yᵉ meeting carried on with prayer.

Fryd., 6. This day Mr. Jn⁰ Walton came to town by request from my former congregation to preach to yᵐ, and to settle among yᵐ, if it might be comfortable. Lord if it be thy holy will give yᵐ new hearts and sincere aims to thy glory in this undertaking, and remove away yᵉ bitter spirit of envy yᵗ is still I fear too much reigning in three or four of yᵐ against me, and forgive yᵐ and me also for Christ's sake.

Lord's D., 8. This day Mr. Jnᵒ Walton preached to my former congregation. This night he lodged at my house.

Tuesd., 10. This day Mr. Jnᵒ Walton preached a lecture in yᵉ meeting house. I am sure I desire yᵉ Lord might direct him what to do. Things respecting his settlement with yᵐ appear strange to me at this time.

Thirsd., 12. Preached; Mr. Wightman absent.

Lord's D., 15. Mr. Walton preached again to my former congregation. That wʰ is of God will stand; but if it be not of God, in his own time it will be brought to naught. Lord I pray thee to enable me to stand still and see the working of thy holy Providence. Fortifie me wᵗʰ all suitable grace and thy name shall be glorified.

Wednesd., 17. This night Mr. Jnᵒ Callender lodged at my house and had suitable opportunity for conference.

Lord's D., 22. This day I preached at Mr. Thomas Stevens's house.

Mond., 23. This day I began to keep school.

Mond., 30. This day I had a number of verses printed for children, 400. Cost 26s.

Thirsd., April 2. I wrote a letter to Mr. Nathˡ Jenkins,[178] minister at Cohansey. This day being a day of prayer in yᵉ Massachusetts, I heard Mr. Clap preach in his house from Ps. 79 : 8, 9 verses, excellently well.

Saturd., 4. Attended church meeting. Prayed with Dr. Arnold's little daughter.

Saturd., 18. This day yᵉ 7th Day Congregation met in my old meeting house.

About this time I received a letter from Mr. Paul Palmer, minister in North Carolina together wᵗʰ a manuscript for yᵉ press, entitled Christ the Predestinated and Elected.

The form of the Agreement of the Baptist church on Rhode Island when they built a meeting house (owning yᵉ Doctrine of

---

[178] Nathaniel Jenkins was born in Wales in 1678; emigrated to this country, and settled at Cape May, New Jersey, in 1712; in 1730 became pastor at Cohánsey, where he died in 1754.

Gen¹ Redemption, under the pastoral care of Mr. James Clarke and Daniel Wightman):

Whereas it hath pleased Almighty God to put it into our hearts, viz., James Clarke, Daniel Wightman, Jeremiah Clarke, [178¼] John Odlin, and the rest mentioned in the instrument above written, bearing date January ye 23, 1706-7 to purchase the land in the said instrument for ye use and service of God and have good and lawful right thereunto and full power in ourselves to order and perpetuate the same to future generations forever. In pursuance thereof we the above s^d purchasers are mutually and unanimously agreed and resolved on ye settlement of s^d lands to ourselves and successors forever in manner and form following : First, we deem, as it is to be understood, these only our successors who are in the same faith and practice as we are now in as may be seen in ye 2^d Article of the Agreement.

1. That James Clarke and Jno Rhodes above named were chosen by s^d purchasers to build a meeting house on s^d lands, who have accomplished ye same, defraying ye charge thereof with money gathered amongst ye purchasers of ye land whereon it now stands.[178½]

[178¼] Jeremiah Clarke, second son, I suppose, of Jeremiah Clarke, one of the signers of the original compact, and brother of Walter Clarke, so long prominent in the public affairs of the colony ; " was deputy from Newport from 1696 to 1705 inclusive, and otherwise is not prominent in the public records. His progeny is exceedingly numerous, and includes among others the family of the late Audley Clarke, Esq., with Gardners, Fowlers, etc., from Newport; and of Providence, several of the oldest and best known families."—Dr. Henry E. Turner, who has given an extended notice of " Jeremy Clarke's family," in the *Newport Hist. Magazine*, Vol. I., pp. 75-96, 129-155.

[178½] Mr. Comer says this was the first meeting house the church had, and he thinks it was built at the time the first purchase of land was made, namely, in 1697. He says: " The land on which the meeting house now standeth [1729] was made over to ye church by Mr. James Clarke, Pastor ; who obtained ye deed thereof in his own name, October the 23d, 1697. In which year the first meeting house was built." He then gives the following: " To all Christian people to whom the present Instrument may come. I James Clarke of Newport on Rhode Island in ye Colony of Rhode Island and Providence Plantations &c., Coopper, [*i. e.*, cooper, by trade,] sendeth greetings. Know ye y^t whereas I said James Clarke did buy or purchase a certain piece of land lying and being in ye town of Newport afores^d containing 30 foot from North to South and from East to West and is bounded Easterly on a highway, Northerly and Westerly on Nathl Coddington's land, Southerly by a piece of land left out for a highway, all which lot or land was bought by me s^d Clarke of Major Nathl Coddington, together with all ye rights and privileges thereunto belonging as is set forth more at large and will more fully appear by ye deed thereof bearing date October ye 23^d, 1697, reference thereunto being had. . . . as also another piece of land containing 30 feet in length and 40 feet in width, and part of s^d purchase is a certain gore containing 8 feet in breadth, and is butted and bounded Northerly on s^d Coddington's land, Easterly on a highway and land already in possession of s^d Clarke, and Westerly on land of s^d Clarke's, and Southerly on a way, as may more fully appear by a deed for ye same bearing date March ye 23^d, 1703-4, reference thereto being had. Know ye y^t I James Clarke do hereby declare and publish that ye money y^t did purchase both pieces of land was contribution money given by certain brethren (hereafter named) to build a meeting house on for the worship and service of God, and for ye accommodation of the same ; And do declare y^t I James Clarke have but an equal right or privilege with ye rest of my brethren hereafter named, and for ye weakening, cutting off, and nulifying, any right, titles or just claim y^t

2. By faith and practice with us, we mean and intend those that are dipped into water with a verbal demonstration of their faith and repentance, yielding obedience to all ye rest of the ordinances of our Lord Jesus Christ, as laying on of hands with a real faith in ye Resurrection of ye dead, and ye Eternal Judgment; as also keeping their holy union and fellowship in Breaking of Bread and Prayer; as will be better seen and is set forth more at large in a printed sheet or declaration of faith and practice of ye Baptized churches, falsely called Anabaptist, in London and in other places in England; w^h sheet is signed by certain Elders and Brethren of s^d churches to ye number of 73, and printed in ye year 1691.

3. We signifie by these presents y^t we are mutually agreed y^t if ourselves ye purchasers of ye land mentioned for holy use in ye instrument above written bearing date January ye 23, 1706-7, and likewise mentioned in ye present discourse,—we say if we ourselves or our successors shall by ye baptized ch [urch] or churches in faith and practice above s^d be censured and judged erroneous or corrupt in principle or practice, in life and conversation, and so by sentence of s^d church be cut off from society and fellowship of ye same, that any and every person or persons so offending shall forever lose his or their claim to any part of ye said land or house.

4. We do hereby oblige ourselves and successors forever, to make and maintain all ye fence y^t ye above named James Clarke was obliged to make and maintain about s^d meeting house lands as may appear by ye two deeds thereof from Major Nath[1] Coddington to ye above s^d James Clarke. In witness whereof and for ratification of each and every of the said mentioned

---

myself or heirs may at any time pretend to by virtue of ye two deeds above mentioned I the s^d James Clarke do hereby in consideration of ye above s^d contribution-money; give, grant in fee, and confirm both ye above s^d deeds of land, together with all ye rights and privileges thereunto belonging, unto my brethren, Jeremiah Clarke, Daniel Wightman, John Odlin, John Greenman, James Brown, John Hammet, Jeremiah Weeden, Joseph Card, James Barker, William Rhodes, Stephen Weeden, William Grinman, Henry Clarke, John Rhodes, and their successors forever, to have and to hold said lands as they are butted and bounded with all ye rights and privileges thereunto belonging; to ye proper use and behoof of all ye above named brethren, for ye use above s^d from him s^d Clarke, his heirs, executors, administrators, or assigns, forever, being freely and clearly acquitted and discharged from all manner of gifts, grants, thirds, jointers, or any incumbrance whatsoever by him s^d Clarke done or made, or suffered to be made at any time before the insealing and delivery hereof and y^t ye s^d Clarke hath good right and lawful power in himself to make sale and good title as above s^d. In witness whereof I have hereunto set my hand and seal this 23d day of January 1706-7.

JAMES CLARKE.

"Witnesses, { JOHN OSBAND,
             { ELIZABETH WILLIAMS.

"Personally appeared before me this 6th of Feb., 1706-7, James Clarke ye subscriber hereof and did own and acknowledge ye above written instrument to be his act and deed.

Attested: JOHN ROGERS, Justice of Peace."

John Comer, in Records of Second Baptist Church, Newport.

particulars, each and every purchaser and proper owner of s⁽ᵈ⁾ lands have set to their hands and fixed their seals this 23rd day of January, 1706-7.

JAMES CLARKE,
JEREMIAH CLARKE,
DANIEL WIGHTMANN,
JOHN ODLIN,
JAMES BARKER,
JEREMIAH WEEDEN,
JOSEPH CARD,
JOHN GREENMAN,
STEPHEN HOOCKEY,

PELEG PECKCOM,
HENRY CLARKE,
JOSEPH WEEDEN,
TIMOTHY PECKCOM,
JOHN RHODES,
JAMES BROWN,
JOHN HAMMETT,
WILLIAM RHODES.

Before us witnesses

WILLIAM DYRE,
JOB BENNETT.

Saturd., May 2. This day I wrote Christian Musto's will.

Tuesd., 5. This day I visited my friends at Swanzey.

Thirsd., 7. This day Sarah Andross was Baptized by Mr. Ephraim Wheaton. I attended yᵉ meeting at Swanzey.

Saturd., 9. Returned home well. I and my wife were sworn at yᵉ Ferry by G. Thomas, yᵗ we had not been to Boston in seven days. Note, he is set there by yᵉ authority on yᵉ account of yᵉ small pox.

Lord's D., 10. This day preached in course. Mr. Staples sent a note to Mr. Wightman, as underwritten; yᵉ reason was because yᵉ young man laid his death to his charge for he had beat and abused him sadly.

MR. WIGHTMAN,

SIR: It is my desire you will appear at yᵉ opening of yᵉ body of Jonathan Lock, this day deceased, and there to put up your prayers to Almighty God to give yᵉ jurors a true sight of yᵉ case, and yᵗ they may be directed by yᵉ Divine Spirit to make a true report of yᵉ cause of his death. So prays your petitioner,

THOMAS STAPLES.

The jurors are warned at one of yᵉ clock. The jury upon search cleared Mr. Staples and brought in yᵗ he died a natural death.

Tuesd. 19. This day I wrote a letter to Mr. Andrew Gifford,[179] Baptist minister in Bristol in Old England, by Mr. Caleb Blenman; yᵉ first [second?] of Croscombe in Somersetshire.

---

[179] Andrew Gifford was born in Bristol England, August 17, 1700; educated at the Bristol Academy. At about the age of twenty-four became assistant pastor in Nottingham; afterwards for two years held the same relation to the Rev. Bernard Foskett, of Bristol.

Fryd., 22. This day the town was mightily alarmed by ye death of a stranger at ye house of Mays Nichols, tavern-keeper, who had been drooping several days; but it appeared to those y^t inspected the body to be ye small pox of w^h he died. By order of authority he was wth utmost despatch buried. It isn't known who he is, or certainly whence he came. His companion is fled out of town to avoid examination, as is probable. The man came last Friday. Lord fit ye town for ye visitation of ye small pox.

A few epitaphs which I took off of some graves in the common burying place at Newport on Rhode Island.

On Mr. Simeon Parrett, who died May 23, 1718, aged 84 years.

>Here doth Simeon Parrett lye,
>Whose wrongs did for vengeance cry,
>But none could have;
>And now ye grave
>Keeps him from injury.

On Mrs. Abigail Wanton, who died May 12, 1726, aged 28 years.

>If tears alas could speak a husband's wo,
>My verse would straight in plentiful numbers flow;
>Or if so great a loss deplored in vain
>Could solace so my throbing heart from pain
>Then could I O sad consolation chuse
>To soothe my careless grief a private muse;
>But since thy well known piety demands
>A public monument at thy George's hands,
>O Abigail, I dedicate this tomb to thee,
>Thou dearest half of poor forsaken me.

On Mr. Willm Sanford, A. M., who died Apr. 24, 1721, aged 31 years.

>Here lyeth dust that as we trust
>United is to Christ,
>Who will it raise, the Lord to praise
>Joined to a soul now blest;

February 5, 1729, he became pastor of the church in Little Wild street, London; became celebrated for his exact and extensive knowledge of ancient manuscripts; in 1757 appointed assistant librarian of the British Museum, though still continuing to discharge the duties of his pastorship; he died June 19, 1784. Dr. Gifford's "collection of rare coins was the most valuable in Great Britain; it attracted the attention of George II., who purchased it for his own cabinet."—Cathcart, *Bap. Ency.*

>With holy ones, placed on bright thrones,
>Crowned with eternal joys,
>In heaven to sing, to God our King,
>Their thankful songs always.

On Mr. John Rogers, who died August ye 11th, 1727, ag. 59, wanting 15 d.

>In his Redeemer's arms he fell asleep,
>Having committed all for him to keep,
>Until ye resurrection morn be come,
>When all ye saints shall fully be brought home
>With saints and angels to eternity

On Mr. Saml Cranston, Esq, Govr of ye Colony, who died Apr. ye 26, 1727, aged 68.

>Rest happie now brave Patriot without end,
>Thy Country's father, and thy Country's friend.

Jno Solomon died May, 1676.
Mr. Willm Hiscox, May 24, 1704, ag. 66.
Mr. Willm Gibson, March 12, 1717. The two last ministers of ye 7th Day church, in Newport.

Fryd., 22. This day news came over from Block Island of [a] most unaccountable piece of wickedness, almost unparalelled, viz: A negro man belonging to Capt. Simon Ray of Block Island being in Newport, in ye heart of ye town, a man being an utter stranger to ye s^d negro gave him a letter and charged him to give it to his master himself, which accordingly he did; and upon his opening it it was a blank, with sundry scabs (as is supposed,) taken from some person sick of ye small pox. In surprise he threw it on ye floor immediately, and ye maid of ye house took it up and burnt it. O w^t wickedness is lodged in ye heart of man. Strict inquiry has been made to find him out, but to no purpose. 'Twas within a week y^t ye letter was sent.

Lord's D., 24. This day preached in course. Mr. Valentine Wightman preached P. M. I wrote a letter to Mr. George Ecclesfield, Baptist minister at Middletown.

Wednesd., 28. This evening Ephraim Broderick having been out about 9 of ye clock, came in, fell into a fit, and fell out of his chair, and in about two hours died so.

Saturd., June 6. This day Mrs. Nichols was removed to Coaster's Harbor, for ye small pox broke out on her.

Lord's D., 7. This day Mr. Saml Maxwell stopt ye church and read a paper to y^m in w^h he signified his intent to lay aside preaching wholly, and y^t he was much in scruple about Infant Baptism. Lord keep those whom I baptized sound in ye faith.

Wednesd., 10. This day died Mrs. Nichols' Indian woman, at Coaster's Harbor, who was carried there on Lord's Day morning with ye small pox. It did not come out well. So ye two first y^t had it died. Lord make it awakening to ye inhabitants.

Thirsd., 11. This day visited Mr. Clap. He informed me of a fast Mr. Adams' people had y^t day week, and y^t they had sent to some ordained ministers to come and help in ye work of ye day; but they refused because they were not clear in ye management of Mr. Adams' dismission, and to some young ministers, who declined because they had heard they intended to try six or eight before a choice, and so declined to stand on ye stool of approbation at Newport; nevertheless two young ministers from ye Massachusetts, and one from Long Island came and carried on the day of fasting by prayer and preaching. Their names were Mr. Cleaverly, Mr. Pearce, Mr. Searing.

So Mr. Clap upon ye refusal of ye ordained ministers, and ye declining of ye young ones, remarked this witty remark on ye people from ye names of ye young ministers. *That they were Cleaverly Pe^rc'd and Sear'd.*

This day also I went to discourse wth Mr. Maxwell about Baptism and so in faithfulness to discharge myself.

Lord's D., 14. This day Mr. Crandall preached to my people, being destitute by reason of Mr. Maxwell's declaring ye Sabbath before for Infant Baptism, or at least his scruples about it.

Lord's D., 21. This day after public service was over in ye town, one Samuel Fenno a printer, lately from Boston, a young man, gathered a number of loose people together at ye house of Jno Pearce and attempted to [do] something by way of preaching from Sol. Song 4 : 7, and sang ye 100 psalm and ye 108 psalm, ye auditory consisting of about a score. Ye principal persons were Mr. Saml Pike, Mr. Brown, Mr. Hawkins, Mr. Johnson, Mr. Martendil &c. Set these aside and there aren't such a number of y^t sort in ye town. Oh profane act, and highly to be disapproved of by all yt wish well to ye interest of Religion. I have done wt lay in my power to suppress it and have brought him to promise to do so no more.

Saturd., 27. This day Mr. Crandall being sick Mr. N. Eyres of New York preached in my old meeting house to his congregation, and in ye P. M. I began ye meeting wth prayer. I have not been in yt pulpit this eighteen months before.

Oh, yt I may be more and more of a forgiving frame of spirit to ym who have grievously injured me. I am afraid I don't forgive ym as I should from my heart, because I can't bear to speak of their actions without a commotion in my own breast.

Lord help me to forgive ym as I expect God for Christ's sake should forgive me.

I found going into ye house affected me and brought things into my mind. I wish it were not so. I think I don't indulge such things. Oh yt I may love ym and forgive and pray more for them.

Lord's D., 28. This evening died Freelove Carr, daughter of Capt. Peleg Carr, about half after ten. She was an amazing instance of sovereign grace and in ye time of her sickness God seemed to ripen her for glory in a wonderful manner. She gave good ground to survivors of her good estate, and with great earnestness of soul she recited to me the twenty-seventh psalm fourth verse.

July. She was buried on Tuesday following from ye meeting house. Mr. Eyres preached. The 7th day meeting house raised that day.

Thirsd., 2. This day Mrs. Claggett was buried from ye meeting house. I preached her funeral [sermon] from Job 19 : 25 according to her own request of me.

Fryd., 3. This day cousin Saml Rogers visited me in deep distress about his soul.

Saturd., 4. This day I was twice sent for to Uncle Rogers' to see Saml. Extremely low about his soul, almost to despair. Preached all day to ye 7th day church upon request, Mr. Crandall sick.

Lord's D., 5. This day preached all day alone, Mr. Wightman at Providence. Sent for after meeting to Uncle Rogers'. Watched there yt night. Lord grant to him under his distress of soul some divine support, ye light of thy reconciled countenance thro Jesus Christ.

This day Mr. J. C. was D. [*Meaning unknown.*]

This day four persons were baptized by Mr. Wightman at Providence.

K

Tuesd., 7. This day ten persons were Baptized by Mr. Wightman at Providence.

May the Lord influence each of them by his Holy Spirit, and give y^m grace to persevere in his ways, and help y^m to adorn the doctrine of God our Saviour in all things.

Thirsd., 9. This day preached; Mr. W. absent.

Saturd., 11. This day preached to ye 7th day congregation.

Mond., 13. Went over to an entertainment at Conanicut.

Tuesd., 14. This day went to see Edward Smith being upon his sick (and I am apt to conclude his death bed); I had no discourse with him as I desired by reason of his being in a kind of lethargy.

Will the Lord give me a truly forgiving frame of spirit as I hope God for Christ's sake will forgive me.

Saturd., 18. This day preached both parts for Mr. Crandall, [he] continuing sick.

Lord's D., 19. Preached in course.

Fryd., 24. This evening an insurrection was made or a mob was raised in the town, occasioned by some young men being put into gaol ye day before for siding and being engaged about a quarrel raised a few evenings before between Augustus Lucas and ——— Coggeshall; ye one calling himself of ye gentleman's party and ye other being lookt upon not so. About twilight the mob began to pull down ye prison fence, so y^t [at] candle light an alarm was beat and men in arms, together wth some of ye authority with drawn swords and other weapons, watched ye prison, for it was threatened to be pulled down y^t night. There was no hurt done in ye insurrection but to one man, Mr. Bassee was knockt down for dead by Richard Durfee wth ye back of a cutlass.

The next day ye men came under bond, and so came out of prison.

August, Wednesd., 5. This day I wrote a letter to Mr. Nathl Jenkins, minister of Cohansey, and Deacon Job Shepherd of ye same place.

Thirsd., 6. This day Jn—r [*name illegible*] upon acknowledgment was received to his place in ye church of Swanzey.

Lord's D., 30. This day I preached at Freetown by request, a large auditory. Returned home well, blessed be God.

Thirsd., Sept. 17. This day [my] former people met at ye meeting house to consult about getting a minister, since Mr.

Jeremiah Condy did not come at the time they expected, and concluded to tarry one week longer.

Fryd., 18. This day Edward Smith died.[180] Lord help me as I hope God for Christ's sake will forgive me.

Sat., 19. This day Mr. Condy[181] came to town to preach to my [former] people by request.

Lord's D., 20. This day Mr. Smith was buried. I was there and attended afternoon exercise in town. Mr. Condy preached to my [former] people. This is the first time they have met in ye meeting house since the 14th of June last. So that it is three months and six days since there was any preaching on ye Lord's Day.

Mond. 21. This day died Mr. Edward Pelham[182] senr. A witty man and a great scholar, but alas too light in his conversation.

Tuesd., Oct. 6. This day I went over to North Kingstown, to see Mr. Paul Palmer, the minister of North Carolina, who was come into ye country to visit ye churches and was returning home by land without coming over to ye

---

[180] Edward Smith, with whom and Samuel Maxwell Mr. Comer's prolonged difficulties seem to have arisen, was a man of decided convictions, and when in the wrong, uncomfortable to get along with. It is by his care, however, that several important items of history have been preserved to us.

[181] Jeremiah Condy was born in 1609; graduated from Harvard College in 1726; after preaching awhile in different places he went to England, whence he was summoned to become pastor of the First Baptist Church in Boston, to which office he was ordained February 14, 1739; the ordination sermon was preached by his friend, the Rev. John Callender, of Newport, which was afterward published at the request of the church. Mr. Condy became an associate member of a society found in Newport to debate questions "in divinity, morality, philosophy, history," etc. Having served the church in Boston as pastor for twenty-five years, he resigned the office in 1764, but continued to reside in that city till his death, August 9, 1768. He was a man "of liberal views, and of an inquisitive and literary taste." Backus speaks of him as "a gentleman of superior powers and learning." Mr. Condy had a son Jeremiah, who was in the book business in Boston, and who published a volume of Dr. Mayhew's sermons in 1755.

[182] Edward Pelham was the son of Herbert, who came with his family from Lincolnshire, England, about the year 1639 or 1640, and who became the first treasurer of Harvard College, holding the office from 1643 to 1650. He was a man of large wealth, holding landed property in both the old and the new world. The son, Edward, was graduated from Harvard in 1673, where he seems to have been a somewhat insubordinate youth; was living in Boston in 1676, where he gave a power of attorney to Samuel Goffe, on the 6th of May of that year; was admitted a freeman at Newport, May 6, 1684; deeded May 28, 1684, twenty-two days after becoming a freeman of Rhode Island, one hundred and twenty acres of land in Cambridge to his *alma mater*; was in 1690 a captain of a Newport military company; never engaged in any business, but lived on his inheritance, and died September 20, 1730. Married in 1693, Freelove, daughter of Benedict Arnold. He had had a wife before, "God's Gift," who may have been another daughter of Arnold—as Arnold had another daughter.

Island by reason of an Act of Assembly prohibiting all from Boston except they lay four days currenteen [quarantine] by reason of the small pox being there. He is a man of parts and worthy.

Wednesd., 7. Returned home well from Narragansett; I praise the holy name of God.

Thirsd., 8. Visited Mr. Condy [he] being sick.

Thirsd., 22. This evening between six and seven of the clock came on the most terrifying awful and amazing Northern light as ever was beheld in New England as I can learn. There was at the bottom of the horizon a very great brightness and over it an amazing red bow extending from North to East like a dreadful fire and many fiery spears, and the East was wonderfully lighted and some part of the appearance continued many hours and people were extremely terrified.

Words can't express ye awfulness of it. W^t God is about [to do] is only known to himself.

Wednesd., Novemb. 4. This night between twelve and one of ye clock a fire broke out at Capt. Malbone's wharf in a cooper shop and prevailed till it had destroyed five or six warehouses and workhouses and one dwelling house and caught another; but thro God's wonderful mercy there were no lives lost, and beyond expectation it was prevented from spreading thro the town.

Lord's D., 8. This day I preached at Freetown, a large auditory. May God bless the journey for the good of precious souls.

About this time I heard of this sad and terrible story. One —— Barter, in Boston, (who in time past I knew well), who was a member of ye New North [Congregational] Church in Boston, under Mr. Thatcher and Mr. Webb's care, who had lately fallen into y^e *prevailing sin of drunkenness;* he was improved by ye church to take care of ye meeting house and to ring ye bell, having once been suspended communion for said sin, but upon acknowledgment and repentance was restored to his place. About a month ago ye deacons of said church having set ye sacramental vessels on ye table in ye meeting house for communion, between ye ringing of ye 1st and 2^d bell, before ye congregation came together he went to ye vessels and drank so excessively y^t he with difficulty got into ye belfry, but was incapacitated upon ye operation of ye drink to perform his office, and lay there *dead drunk* all sermon and sacrament time. Y^e church ye next day call'd a meeting and suspended and admonished him and put him out of his office. Oh, terrible and almost unheard-of wicked action.[182½]

Mond., 23.
This day I wrote a letter to Mr. Jenkins minister at Cohansey, Mr. Eyres minister at New York; and Mr. Davis minister at Trent-town [Trenton] in the Jersies, and Mr. Symmonds minister at South Carolina.

Heard y^t Mr. Henry Loveall[183] was ordained about a month ago by Mr. Palmer minister of North Carolina and Mr. Drake minister at Piscataqua in East New Jersey, colleague with Mr. Drake.

The Lord furnish him wth ministerial gifts and graces and make him an able minister of ye New Testament.

Saturd., 28.
This day Mr. Jeremiah Condy came again to preach to my [former] people by request and to tarry all winter; *it may be*, if ye Lord will.

I want to see in myself more of a forgiving spirit to them than I am afraid I have now.

Lord help me to forgive them; I long to forgive y^m heartily. Oh w^t a spirit have I, too irreconcilable.

Thirsd., Decemb. 3.
This day I received a bequeath of forty shillings from Mr. Daniel Fortinue, which his wife Mrs. Elizth Fortinue desired him to give me to remember her by as a token of love. She died Nov. ye 2^d before.

From ye Gazette, number 572, Novr 30, 1730, there is this admirable relation from London, Sept. 4th, 1730. They write from Cambridge that Dr. Green, of Clare Hall in y^t university, and author of the Greeman[?] Philosophy, who lately died there, has made ye Master with three Fellows of Clare Hall, Dr. Bentley wth three other heads of colleges his Executors, and has bequeathed all his estate to the amount of £2,000 to Clare Hall on ye following conditions:

1. They are to publish all his posthumous works;
2. They are to get his body anatomized and to hang his skeleton at ye head of a class of books which he had presented to ye Hall Library just before he died; he has also ordered monuments

---

[182½] [Unquestionably the wine used at the communion in those days was genuine wine. There was no thought of change suggested even by such an infamous abuse as that here related by Comer; any more than there was, in the mind of Paul, in the case mentioned in 1 Cor. 11 : 20–34. There was no substitution of something else, like that which in our day, in certain churches, has in the judgment of many, effected a mutilation of the ordinance.—J. W. W.]

[183] [Henry Loveall appears to have been an unworthy man—perhaps a "wolf in sheep's clothing."—*See Comer's Diary, pages 114, 117, 118.*—J. W. W.]

to be erected in five several places with long epitaphs he has left inserted on each of y^m. And in case those of Clare Hall do not execute this his will, his effects are to go to St. Ju^d^'s College; and if they refuse, to any other of the respective colleges y^t will undertake its full execution. By ye Journal we learn y^t Clare Hall refuses to do it.

Wednesd., 9. This day received from my dear Brother the Rev^d Mr. Nathl Jenkins two letters to my great satisfaction.

Fryd., 25. This day I wrote a letter to Mr. Andrew Gifford, Baptist minister in Bristol in Old England, and Mr. Joseph Stennett, Baptist minister in Exeter, Old England; the 2^d to each. I informed y^m according to my best knowledge y^t there were 26 Baptist churches in America under their several divisions, and about 2,110 communicants, reckoning from North Carolina to Boston.

Wednesd., 30. I tremble with ye sad news this day I received from Mr. Nicholas Eyres, of New York, dated Novr ye 26, concerning Mr. Henry Loveall, alias Desolate Baker, *i. e.* y^t he served his time on Long Island when he came first from England wth Daniel Sears, . . . y^t he ran away from his master, changed his name, and now lives with another man's wife in adultery. This awful report was made known about a fortnight after his ordination.

I can't say he can in my judgment be ever accepted as a minister, especially when I call to mind 1 Timothy 3 : 7.

Glorious God I beseech thee give divine direction to thy servants in the ministry and to ye church among whom so woful a difficulty hath happened, what to do in this affair so as thy holy name may not be blasphemed and thy cause suffer. Direct by thy spirit and grace, and give true and sound repentance unto him who has so fallen by his ingenuity in ye days of his vanity. Make him a true gospel penitent for Christ's sake.

Thus I end ye year 1730. It has been a year in which I have eyed the divine goodness of my gracious God to me and mine, in providing for me on all accounts, for which all possible praise be rendered to his holy name.

I have been preserved from sickness this year. I have had a competency of the good things of this life. I have been sensibly supported by divine promises as to my inward man.

There have happened this year: One found dead in her bed. The northern light hath appeared this year four times, but the most awful October 22.

An exact account of what I owe in the world this first day of January, 1731. JOHN COMER.

	£	s.	d.
To the Colony................	50	0	0
To Mr. Odlin.................	50	0	0
To sister Elizth Barker.......	40	0	0
To mother Rogers.............	40	0	0
To Mrs. Sarah Collins.........	20	0	0
To Madam Cranston...........	20	0	0
To Arnold Collins.............	20	0	0
To sundry debts to etc........	40	0	0
Total............	280	0	0
So that I have gained this year.........	11	0	0

Fryd. January 1, 1731. This day I begin a new year. Lord grant me new strength to work for thee.

This year if God grant opportunity I purpose to go a journey into the Jersies. May God's name be glorified and souls edified by it; and will God protect and prosper me and return me, and I'll glorifie his name. May God order in his holy providence things comfortable for me and protect and preserve my family in my absence. I commit all to God with my whole heart now this moment y^t I am penning it. Amen.

Mond., 11. Mr. Jeremiah Condy was chosen to office by my former people, tho some were very much dissatisfied in ye choice. Whether he will accept ye call I know not. I pray God to direct him. 'Tis dark to me.

Mond., 25. This day I went to Swanzey and saw Mr. Elisha Callender, of Boston, and discoursed to my satisfaction. Snowy weather. This day was church meeting at Swanzey. In order to accommodate matters about Mr. Jno Callender, in ye church by a major vote he was admitted to preach again.

Tuesd., 26. Went over to Providence. Extremely cold. Tarried at Providence till Friday P. M. Returned yⁿ to Swanzey, and on Saturday evening got safe home. I bless ye Lord for his protection and preservation of me. I had comfort in some dear friends' conversation. I praise ye Lord for every comfort of y^t nature.

Tuesd., March 16. Taken from my Journal y^t I kept while on my journey to Philadelphia. This day set out by water to New York with Mr. Richard Robinson. A snowy time, yᵉ wind at N. E. in yᵉ P. M. Becalmed. Lay to near Watch Point all night. A rolling sea.

Wednesd., 17. About break of day hoisted sail, wind hard at N. N. W. Great sea near Watch Point, like to have been lost on yᵉ rocks. Got into Stoningtown harbor about one P. M. Lodged at Mr. Greenman's. Praised be yᵉ name of yᵉ Lord.

Thirsd., 18. Went aboard in yᵉ morning, hoisted anchor about 9 A. M., wind N. W. Got to N. London about 3 P. M.

Fryd., 19. Remained at New London, wind contrary. Went to visit Mr. Gorton, got to town at night, dark and rainy.

Saturd., 20. Called up about day dawn. Wind at N. N. W. Pleasant morning. Set sail at 6 A. M.; about 12 touched on Seabrook bar; about 2 P. M. anchored at Southhold harbour, by yᵉ oyster ponds on Long Island. Went ashore and tarried till 7, and about 11 at night hoisted anchor and set sail; wind extremely hard, but God preserved.

Lord's D., 21. Becalmed till 1 P. M. At night dropt anchor in yᵉ Sound against Fairfield. A rolling sea.

Mond., 22. This morning about 4 weighed anchor, wind at N. E., rainy, shifted about 9 to S. W., exceeding hard, great sea. About one anchored at White Stone, yᵉ tide not suiting to go thro Hell gate. This day we were in great danger by many squalls. Lodged ashore at Mr. Lawrence's comfortably.

Tuesd., 23. About day dawn went aboard. About 8 went thro Hell gate. About 10 A. M. arrived safe at New York. Thus God has preserved me and I now offer yᵉ praise to him. Waited on Revᵈ Nicholas Eyres. Saw Mr. Jnᵒ Campbell my former acquaintance, kindly treated, took a view of yᵉ city. Went to see yᵉ new Dutch church wʰ is very beautiful, a stone building. It is curiously wrought, being 100 feet in length, and 70 in breadth, having in it 150 pews, and no pillars to support yᵉ roof wʰ is finely arched, having two doors opposite to the pulpit; over each in a fine white stone of about a foot and a half square are these two Scripture epithets at large, Ps. 28 : 8; Isa. 56 : 7. The [steps?] up to ye belfry are 116, 16 windings. Lodged at Mr. Eyres'. Cost me a double bitt.

Wednesd., 24. Remained at York. Mr. Stephens went with me to see the Fort, which is a strong one. Saw yᵉ chapel, yᵉ organs, the Governour's Library, the garden, where I saw peach trees in yᵉ blossom and many delightful varieties. Cost me two bitts.

Thirsd., 25. This evening about 9 the boat presented to go down to Middleton, thirty miles. I went. Anchored at Middleton about two in yᵉ morning. Breakfasted at Mr. Watson's.

Got a horse free to Deacon Mott's, 5 m. Got to his house about nine, kindly treated. Lodged at Mr. Holmes' with yᵉ Revᵈ. Mr. George Ecclesfield, yᵉ minister of yᵉ town.[184]

Fryd., 26. Preached at Middleton in East New Jersie, from 1 Cor. 2 : 2. About 100 auditors. Lodged at Mr. Mott's.

Sat., 27. Rainy. Deacon Moot [Mott] and Mr. Campbell went with me to Piscataqua. Very uncomfortable, got there about dark to Deacon Still's. Lodged there. 22 m.

Lord's D., 28. Preached at Piscataqua [185] by Mr. Henry Loveall's request (who is the minister) from Gal. 6 : 15, having before meeting waited on Elder Drake and Elder Dunham. Note. This church is in utmost confusion on yᵉ account of some evil actions of Mr. Loveall, done before his profession, but lately heard of by yᵐ. A meeting appointed next Friday at 10 of yᵉ clock. Lord overrule all for thy own glory.

Had of Elder Jnᵒ Drake the following letter sent to yᵉ church by the Revᵈ. Mr. Natˡ Jenkins minister at Cohansey.

COHANSEY, Decembʳ yᵉ 26ᵗʰ, 1730.

To the Honoured Jnᵒ Drake, Elder, to the Deacons and yᵉ whole church at Piscataqua owners [owning?] Believers' Baptism, Greeting.

Dearly beloved friends for whom I have great esteem and regard, I wish you all grace and peace thro Jesus Christ our Lord.

Brethren, I am in a straight what or how to write to you. Your presumptuous precipitation in all your proceedings have given me ground to fear yᵗ you are fallen from yᵉ grace of the gospel. You askt my advice and others. We gave it and would have you prove and try your man before you would

---

[184] This town is in Monmouth county two of the patentees of which were Obadiah and Jonathan Holmes, sons of the famous Obadiah Holmes, of Rhode Island. The date assigned to the church is 1688. We are told that "this is the oldest church in the State" of New Jersey. Ecclesfield, the name of the minister is sometimes spelled Eaglesfield. It was, of course, a Baptist church.

[185] A large tract of country east of the Raritan river was purchased of the Indians in 1663, and at one part of it called Piscataway. A church was formed in 1689, "which is the next to Middletown in point of seniority." In this church Henry Loveall was ordained to assist the Rev. John Drake, but he "never administered ordinances; for the vileness of his character was soon discovered."—Benedict, *Hist.*, I., 567.

close with him as your minister; but you neither minded my advice nor y^t of our Association, but as persons infatuated you have rushed on without rule or precedent to ordain a man for ye ministry y^t is hardly fit to be a common or private member. How is it you did not read their qualifications 1 Tim. 3 : 2, 3, 4, 5, 6, 7. Not a novice &c. And he must have a good report of y^m y^t are without. Is it a good report y^t he committed uncleanness? [*Certain particulars omitted.*] And is it a good report that now his last spouse should be another man's wife? [*Certain particulars omitted.*] Is it a good report y^t he was and yet is an impudent liar? And could you be so childish as to be satisfied with a bare confession, and as soon as he had confessed to jump into the pulpit to teach you y^t were never guilty of half his crimes? What is this but as if a criminal would confess his villainy at the bar and as soon as he had done to jump to the bench to give judgment. Oh monstrous! How could you join with such an one without more y^n ordinary humiliation as a common brother! Could any of you think of y^t place 1 Tim. 5 : 22, 24, 25 lay hands suddenly on [no] man &c. What right had *Paul Palmer* to be employed by you in that work? Were there no ministers belonging to your own Association? Only you were afraid you should not be suffered to dance about your calf. But, my dear Brethren, consider the dreadful day of the Lord is coming, and all the churches shall know that he knows their hearts and thoughts. Consider y^t reproach you brought on your profession hereby. I am ashamed of it. I could have told you—[The letter closes thus abruptly.]

16. This day I returned home from visiting the churches. Thanks and praise to God's holy name for Divine preservation.

June 14. This day my second daughter, *Mary*, was born, on Tuesday night about 11 of ye clock. Lord I give it up to thee to thy guidance and government of thy blessed Spirit.

28. On Monday I and my former people met in the meeting house and accommodated our old difference. [185½]

[185½] This reconciliation between Mr. Comer and the church was two years after his dismission. The *Church Records* give an account of a meeting June 28, 1731, "gathered at the request of Mr. Comer, and by consent of our Elder, William Packcom." "After some discourse with Mr. Comer concerning the difference that has been a long time between him and the church, Mr. Comer being sensible of his mistakes desired forgiveness, and in particular his timing of that discourse concerning laying on of hands, and in a sermon which he afterwards preached, which was very offensive to the church, charging them with such crimes as they were no ways sensible they were ever guilty of, which he desired might be overlookt. And it was agreed that all papers that were written on both sides relating to the difference, might be produced and burnt, which was accordingly done; and the meeting finished in love and peace, with prayer by Mr. Comer." Herein Mr. Comer shows his truly Christian spirit. He was about to leave Newport for another field of labor, and could not depart until a reconciliation had been effected; and he evidently went as far as he consistently could in making concessions to secure the end he sought, but sacrificing no conviction or principle.

Sat., July 8. This day I desired a dismission from ye church where I had preached for more yn two years, because I was never settled there and found yt some could not bear my preaching ye doctrines of grace, they being a Genl church,—which I obtained.

19. This day by a letter from Rehoboth I was invited there to preach, which invitation I complied with.

Lord's D., Aug. 1. This day I am 27 years of age. Lord grant me grace to serve thee this year also to the glory of thy holy name.

Thirsd., 12. This day I removed my family to Rehoboth in the Massachusetts Province. Got safe there, blessed be God.

The last of this month the steeple of the church at N. port was set on fire with lightning, and a quarter of the spire was forced to be cut down to prevent the whole building from being consumed.

And about ye same time, in Boston, one Capt. Sam, an Indian sachem, was killed by his horse throwing him and breaking his neck in ye street.

Tuesd., Sept., 20. This evening about 7 appeared an awful Northern Light with some bright streamers in it.

Wednesd., Oct. 13. This day Mr. Jno. Callender[186] was ordained over my former flock at Newport, on Rhode Island. Mr. Elisha Callender, of Boston, and Mr. Saml Maxwell performed the service.

Saturd., 23. This day I preached at N. port in ye 7th day congregation.

Wednesd., 27. This day I bought a house of Mr. Jonathan Norton in Rehoboth, and the deed was signed. I am to give him 90 pounds within three years.

---

[186] The pastoral service thus entered upon, which was to prove so important to the church, was destined to continue until the death of Mr. Callender, which occurred January 26, 1748. Mr. Callender took a deep interest in the public schools of Newport; was a member of the philosophical society which was afterwards developed into the Redwood Library and Athenæum; preached several sermons that were published: one to young men, one at the funeral of the Rev. Nathaniel Clap, one at the ordination of the Rev. Jeremiah Condy; but the one most celebrated was a historical discourse delivered in 1738, the centennial anniversary of the settlement of Rhode Island; it was the first history of the State ever written, and to it subsequent writers have been greatly indebted. The Rhode Island Historical Society republished the discourse in 1838, and prefixed to it a memoir of the author prepared by the Rev. Romeo Elton, D. D. While residing in Swanzey, just before his ordination at Newport, Mr. Callender, on the 15th of February, 1730, married Elizabeth Hardin of the former place, by whom he had six children. See also note 70.

Mond., Novr. 15. This day a Baptist meeting house was raised in Rehoboth.

1732. Saturday, January 1 This day I begin a new year in a new place, tho not in a new employment; for my delight of soul is in serving my dear Redeemer in the sacred service of the ministry which I prefer and esteem above and beyond everything else (tho I acknowledge unfit, unworthy in myself). Lord who is sufficient for these things? Sufficiency is alone of God, on him I rest and rely continually. Lord grant me this year new supplies of thy Spirit; and as I now [have] a new year I entreat I may find my desires renewed to glorify and serve thee.

Lord's D., 16. This day Mr. Jnº Luther's house was burnt down about 11 of yᵉ clock A. M. in Swanzey.

Thirsd., 20. This day a Baptist church was gathered in Rehoboth, and I was chosen to the pastoral office.[187]

---

[187] While this church formed in Rehoboth was in its *order* "Six Principle," it was in its doctrine "Calvinistic"; it was modeled on the pattern of the churches in Philadelphia, whence Mr. Comer had just returned from a visit, giving expression to his "great satisfaction in the sight beheld of the faith and order of those churches." [Namely, churches of the Philadelphia Baptist Association.—J. W. W.] The change of sentiments which occasioned the severance of his first pastoral relations in Newport, embraced nothing more than the tenet "of imposition of hands." See the entry in the Diary under date July 3, 1731.

[Here ends the work of annotation by the late lamented Dr. Barrows. It may be proper to add a few words to this, his last note. Mr. Comer appears to have severed his pastoral relation with the First Church, Newport, because he believed in and advocated "the imposition of hands on the newly baptized," they and he alike being "Calvinists." And later he severed his relations with the Second or "six principle" Church, because though he and they alike believed in and practiced "the imposition of hands," they were generally "Arminian" in sentiment, and he "Calvinistic." Hence his satisfaction expressed with the faith and order then existing in the Philadelphia Association—the oldest Association in America—is easily understood. The churches of that body held the "Calvinistic doctrine" with great tenacity, and also practiced "the imposition of hands." This ancient custom has gone out of use, in the course of time, among American Baptists, except in a few churches. It has been superseded by the "right hand of fellowship," [or, "of welcome"]. In a few churches the old practice is still retained. They do not make it a "term of communion," or a subject of contention with their brethren, but are unwilling to abandon a rite which seems to them so scriptural and so significant of the gift of the Holy Spirit promised to the believer. With some of these, the "hand of fellowship" follows. Others consider this unnecessary, there being no scriptural authority for it, so far as newly baptized converts are concerned; while the "laying on of hands," accompanied by solemn prayer, seems to them far superior in meaning and impressiveness. The "imposition" or "laying on of hands" is now practiced by the Second and the Roxborough Baptist churches of Philadelphia, and until recently also by the Lower Merion Baptist Church, in the vicinity of Philadelphia. It is retained in the Second Baptist Church of Newport, which has now nothing else in common with the "Six Principle Baptists," but is in fellowship with the Regular Baptists of Rhode Island. Whether the practice is found now in any other regular Baptist churches in the Philadelphia Association or elsewhere in America, I cannot say. But if we may judge from the Philadelphia Confession of Faith, and from notices in this diary and elsewhere, it was once a part of acknowledged order

Wednesd., 26.	This day I was publicly installed pastor over yᵉ Baptist church in Rehoboth, the Elders and Messengers of yᵉ church of Swanzey assisted. Elder Ephraim Wheaton preached from 1 Thess. 5 : 12, 19, and gave me *the right [hand] of fellowship.*
Lord's D., February 13.	This day I preached at Newport for Mr. John Callender in my old congregation, it being yᵉ first time since we parted.
Mond., 14.	This night about 11 of yᵉ clock Mr. Hugh Cole, Jun., lost [by fire] his house and everything belonging to him in it save his family, who narrowly escaped (thro God's distinguishing goodness), some in part, and others not at all in clothes, in an extreme cold night in Swanzey.
Tuesd., 15.	This day for yᵉ extremity of cold may deserve to be chronicled.
Lord's D., 20.	This day about 1 P. M. my wife's mother Mrs. Sarah Rogers departed this life and I have ground to hope she died in yᵉ Lord.
Lord's D., March 27.	This day A. M. another house was burnt in Swanzey. This day in the town of Rehoboth one *Joshua Abel* cut his own throat with a razor about sunrise. He had been ill in body some time.
Wednesd., April 5.	This day a remarkable snow fell between two and three feet deep, the deepest we had this year.
Fryd, June 16.	This day upon request I with three Brethren went on to visit some Baptized persons at Sutton and Leicester.
Lord's D., 18.	I baptized at Sutton four persons, three men and one woman, viz. Thomas Richardson, Daniel Dennee, Elisha Nevers, Martha Green.
May 1, 1733.	I being now weak in body [¹⁸⁸] think it not amiss to set down an account of my worldly affairs, how far I

---

among regular American Baptists generally, and was by no means peculiar to the "Six Principle Baptists," whose sentiments were Arminian, and (as I suppose) are so still. I am free to say that I wish the ancient custom could be restored in all our Baptist churches.—J. W W.]

[188] [The date of this entry is about a year earlier than that of Mr. Comer's death. The weakness of which he complains was probably from the effects of the disease which cut short his days. "Rehoboth is a large town, extending from Taunton and Dighton to Providence, about twelve miles; and in 1791, there were four thousand seven hundred and ten persons therein, and ten religious societies, which is more than we have in any other town of their numbers, in these parts. Cruel oppression on the one hand, and an abuse of

lately went in clearing my debts when I sold my house to Mr. Isaac Peckcom in Newport, April ye 6th, 1733, in which sale I met with ye most heavy loss of all, selling for just 100 pounds less than I was offered about three years before, ye times being dead and money scarce. However I brought my affairs into a less compass, viz. April ye 7th, 1733 cleared ye 50 pound bond of Mr. Odlin.

Cleared ye 50 pound bond of Capt. Peckcom's to ye Colony.

Cleared ye 20 pound bond of Mrs. Sarah Collins.

Paid 18 pound[s] to Mr. Arnold Collins.

Paid 10 pound[s] to Madam Cranston.

A record of marriages performed by John Comer, pastor of the Baptist church in the town of Rehoboth, in the province of ye Massachusetts Bay in N. England.

1732. On Friday night, June ye 30th, 1732, Mr. John Davis of Haverhill was married to Mrs. Sarah Barney of Rehoboth, certificates of their legal publication from under ye clerk's hand being produced. 10s. John Eaton, clerk of Haverhill, Ezek. Read, clerk of Rehoboth.

On Thursday evening, September ye 14th, 1732, Mr. Jeremiah Ormsbee, Jr., and Mrs. Peirsee Millard, both of Rehoboth, produced a certificate of their legal publication were married by me. 10s. Ezek. Read, clerk of Rehoboth.

The above sent and recorded in ye Town Record, Octr ye 12th, 1732.

On October ye 19th, 1732, Caleb Salsbury and Prudence West were married in Rehoboth by me, upon producing legal certificates. 5s. Hez^h Luther, clerk of Swanzey, Ezek. Read, clerk of Rehoboth.

---

liberty on the other, have been the cause of it. Many had joined with the Baptists of Swanzey, from time to time, until Mr. John Comer came and assisted in forming a church in Rehoboth. . . . He was an excellent preacher of the gospel, and an eminent instrument of reviving doctrinal and practical religion in Newport, for six years before he removed to Rehoboth, in August, 1731; and a Baptist church was formed there January 20, 1732, and he became their pastor, and it increased to ninety-five members in less than two years. And in that time he went and labored in Sutton, Leicester, Middleborough, and other places. But he exerted his powers so much in this noble cause, that he fell into a consumption, and died joyfully, May 23, 1734, before he was thirty years old. His son is now a member of the Baptist church in Warren [R. I.], and he lent me his father's diary and other writings, which have been very serviceable in our history."—Backus *History, Weston's Edition*, II., 436. Elsewhere Backus remarks of Comer's labors in Rehoboth "But how much did he do in a little time!" (II., 31.) Fitting words wherewith to close what my beloved friend Dr. Barrows has written to elucidate and illustrate THE DIARY OF JOHN COMER.—J. W. W.]

1732-33. On February ye 22^d, 1732-33, Joseph Salsbury and Eliz^th Round were married by me in Rehoboth, upon producing a legal certificate. 5s. Ezek. Read, clerk.

1733. On April ye 19th, 1733, Elijah Horton and Mehitable Richman were married by me in Rehoboth, upon producing legal certificates. 5s. Ezek. Read, clerk.

April ye 26th, 1733, Jabez Round and Renew Carpenter were married by me in Rehoboth, upon producing legal certificates. 10s.

May ye 17th, 1733, William Saben and Phebe Eddy were married by me in Rehoboth, upon producing a legal certificate. 10s.

May ye 22^d, 1733, Thomas Jollas and Mehitable Ormsbee were married by me in Rehoboth, upon producing legal certificates. 10s.

June ye 11th, 1733, Thomas Peck and Mary Kingsley were married by me in Rehoboth, upon producing legal certificates. 10s. The above entered on ye Town Records.

Novr ye 11th, 1733, Abijah Luther and Prudence Peck were married by me in Rehoboth. 6s.

Decemb^r ye 20th, 1733, Benjn Hix and Ann Ormsbee were married by me in Rehoboth.

1734. March ye 27th, 1734, Stephens Jennings and Mary Horton were married by me in Rehoboth.

An extract out of Swanzey church book, page 227: Sept. 2^d, 1725, Mr. John Comer was chosen to assist Elder Ephraim Wheaton in the work of the gospel ministry.

The names of the committee chosen by the church to treat with him:

JOHN EASTERBROOK,
BENJ. COLE,
JOHN WEST,
HUGH COLE,
EPHRAIM MARTIN,
JONATHAN KINGSLEY,
RICHARD KARDIN.

An account of such persons that have been Baptized by Mr. John Comer, in remote places from my habitation for the year 1732.

Sutton, June 18, 1732.	Thomas Richardson, Daniel Dennee. Elijah Nevers, Martha Green.
Leicester, June 20, 1732.	Joshua Nichols, Abiathar Vinton. Bathsheba Nevers, Lydia Vinton.
Middleborough, July 17.	Benjamin Booth.
Barrington, July 20, 1732.	Levi Luther, Elizth Martin.
Nov. 30, 1732.	Jonathan Cole, Ebenezer Cole. Elizth Cole, Obadiah Bowen.

The six last to join with ye church in Swanzey.

SUPPLEMENTARY NOTE.

Since the preparation of this work for the press, there has come into my hands a written sketch of Rev John. Comer, by Miss Annie E. Cole, dated Warren, R. I., May, 1888. From this I make the following extracts:

"During these years [the two years or more at Rehoboth] Mr. Comer[1] preached, wrote, and studied, but consumption, a hereditary disease, now claimed him for its victim. He died May 23, 1734, in the thirtieth year of his age, and was buried by the side of the Rev. Ephraim Wheaton, in the rural cemetery where Mr. Wheaton was laid to rest one month before.

"Mr. Comer left a widow and three children, John, Sarah, and Mary. John, the eldest, married Elizabeth, daughter of Thomas and Sarah [Bosworth] Kinnicutt. He was a zealous Baptist and a constituent member of the Warren Church in 1761. He was also one of the three who, in behalf of the new church, presented the ordination call to the Rev. James Manning to become the first pastor. He lived to be upward of ninety years of age and died December 30, 1816, closing in peace a blameless and worthy life. His descendants still own and occupy the homestead lands of their venerable ancestor.

"The daughters of Rev. John Comer, Sarah and Mary, married into Rehoboth families, Mendal and Cranston, and their paternal name was soon lost.

"Mrs. Sarah [Rogers] Comer, [widow of our John Comer], married for her second husband Samuel Millard or Miller, a prominent and wealthy citizen of Swanzey and an early inhabitant of Warren, when the final settlement of boundary lines in 1746 gave this new township to Rhode Island.

---

[1] Miss Cole says the name is now written and pronounced "Coomer."

He was grandfather of Gen. Nathan Miller, a general in the Revolution and member of the Continental Congress in 1785. Samuel Millard died in 1748 and his widow survived him ten years, departing this life in 1758, in her fifty-third year.

"The Rev. Dr. Wm. Rogers, successor to the Rev. Morgan Edwards in the pastorate of the Philadelphia church, who was also, and for a short time, the only pupil in the Rhode Island College [now Brown University] and said to be, at the time of his death in 1824, the last remaining chaplain of the Revolutionary army, was a member of the family to which Mrs. Comer belonged, and during his collegiate course made his home with the son, Mr. John Comer, at the family residence on Bristol Neck, now South Warren.

"The Rev. John Comer ranked among the cultured men of his age and his piety was deep, fervent, and active. He possessed decided literary talents and designed writing a history of the Baptists in America; he had commenced gathering materials for that purpose, had visited Philadelphia, and opened an extensive correspondence abroad, when his far-reaching plans and proposed labors were closed by death.

"The local historians tell us that Mr. Comer was curious in noting all the remarkable events that came within his knowledge, and the two manuscript volumes [of his diary] of the Rhode Island Historical Society are but a small portion of his writings, for the centuries lay vandal hands upon manuscripts and unbound memoranda. Nor can, or ought, his talents and abilities to be judged by these fragmentary notes, never intended for the public eye, far less for the criticism of future generations. Yet through the intervening century and a half the Baptist church historians of New England have gathered strength and inspiration, as well as facts, from the Diary of John Comer, though he died before his literary life was fairly begun."

The second volume of the two, above referred to, consists chiefly of memoranda and records which the Rhode Island Historical Society's Committee thought it unnecessary to print in full. The most important have been, I think, incorporated in the Diary [Ms. Vol. I.] by Dr. Barrows at the proper places. There is also a statement of the religious belief of John Comer, "delivered publicly" by him "on the day of [his] ordination," which it was also thought unnecessary to give. His views, it is well known, were those of the Regular or Calvinistic Baptists of his day, including the tenet that the imposition of hands on the newly baptized is obligatory. What those views were are clearly set forth in the "Confession of Faith" of the Philadelphia Baptist Association, 1742. This may be found in Cathcart's *Baptist Encyclopedia*, pp. 1311 fl.

Cathcart, in the *Baptist Encyclopedia*, p. 255, pays this tribute to John Comer:

"Mr. Comer was the most remarkable young man in the Baptist history of New England, and his early death was a calamity to the churches in that section of that country, suffering at the time so severely from Puritan persecutions and needing so much his unusual talents and acquirements."

I am happy to be able to put on record the additional facts and the just testimonies contained in this note. For the rest—all that has passed into oblivion—we must wait till the day of the Lord's coming, when all his faithful servants will receive full credit and full reward, through abounding and sovereign grace.—J. W. W.

INDEX TO DIARY.

INCLUDING INTRODUCTION AND SUPPLEMENTARY NOTE.

(Figures refer to pages of this volume.)

Accidents recorded, 17, 24, 36, 43, 47, 50, 54, 55, 56, 57, 63, 66, 83, 87, 92, 97, 100, 112, 119, 120, 121.
Adams, Rev. John, 45, 49-54, 101, 108.
Appleton, Nathaniel, D. D., 33.
Association, Baptist: ("Six-Principle") 66-70, 78, 81; Letter of, to South Kingston Church, 81; Philadelphia, 125.
Aurora Borealis, 55, 65, 95, 100, 112, 114.

Baptism: infant, 26, 108; believers', 26.
Baptist Churches Mentioned: Boston, First, 32, 69; Cohansey, 102; Dartmouth, 68; Groton, 68; Middletown, 107, 117; New London, 42, 67; Newport, First, 36, 40, 57 ff., 69, 118, 119; Newport, Second, 40, 69 ff., 102 ff.; Newport, Seventh Day, 40, 70; Newport, Mr. White's, 41; New York, 67; North Kingston, 69; Philadelphia, First, 125: Piscataqua (Piscataway), 117; Rehoboth, 120 ff.; Providence (several), 66-68, 95; South Carolina, 95; South Kingston, 68, 81; Swanzey (two), 34, 69 ff., 95, 96, 101; Trenton, 113; Warren, 124; Westerly (Seventh Day), 70; Warwick, 69.
Baptist Principles, Polity and Practice, 9, 11; Arminianism, 7, 69; Associations, 66, 68, 78, 79-81, 125; baptism, 26, 27, 104, 108; Church and State, 86; communion, 43, 79, 104; discipline, 58, 93; dismission of members, etc., 38, 92, 119; doctrines of grace, 7, 119, 125; helping others, 45; imposition of hands, 7, 40, 57, 59, 104, 125; meeting houses, 103-105, 120; minister, wicked, 114, 117, 118; ministry, the, 37, 38, 120, 121; missionary work, 45, 46; ordination, 39, 42, 63, 113, 119; Philadelphia Association, 125; reception of members, 77, 78, 98; singing, 58; support of pastors, 43, 58.
Baptists: "Calvinistic" churches of, in New England, 69; church difficulties among, 7, 35, 55, 57, 58, 59, 94, 96, 98, 100-102, 109-111, 113, 118, 119; in North Carolina, letter from, 84; persecutions of (and others), 8, 62, 75, 76, 79, 80; in South Carolina, write, 85; statistics of, in America, 68-70, 85, 114.
Barnard, Rev. John, 30-32.
Barrows, C. E., D. D., author of "Development of Baptist Principles in R. I.," 11; editor of this work, 9-11; pastor of John Comer's church, 10; sketch of, 11-13.
Berkeley, Dean, George, 60, 71.
Boston: great fire in, 16; night watch in, 78.
Brown, Jonathan, case of, 84, 93.
Burnoll, Rebecca, 32.
Burnett, Gov. William, 54, 79.

Callender, Rev. Elisha: letter to Comer, 36.
Callender, Rev. John: mentioned, 101, 115; ordained over First Newport Church, 119.
Cambridge: school at, 24; First Congregational Church of, 26.
Carr, Freelove: happy death of, 109.
Clarke, Rev. John: spoken of, 10; persecuted in Boston, 75, 76.
Clap, Rev. Nathaniel: spoken of, 49-54; wise words of, 94; pun by, 108.
Claggett, William, 100.
Cold, great, 121.
Comer, John, Rev.: acceptance of call to First Newport, 37, 38; accounts (money matters), 58, 59, 72, 91, 98, 99, 115, 121, 122; ancestry, 15, 16, 58; apprenticeship, 18, 19; autograph of, 15; Backus' account of, 7, 8; baptism, exercised about, 26, 30; baptisms by, 43, 48, 57, 58, 77, 78, 98, 121, 124; baptized, 7, 32; Barrows, C. E., D. D., edits his diary, 9-11; bequest to, 113; birth, 7, 15; Boston, returns to, 32; builds a house, 54, 55; buried, 124; buys a house, 119; call to Newport, First, 36; Cathcart's estimate

of, 125; children of, 44, 54, 59, 118, 124; Cole, Miss Annie E., her sketch of Comer, 124, 125; Congregationalist, originally a, 7, 25, 26; conviction and conversion of, 17, 18, 20, 22, 24, 25; death of, 8, 124; depressed in spirits, 91; descendants of, 124; dismissed from Boston church, 38, from First Newport, 59; from Second Newport, 119; Diary his, character of, 8, 9; value of, 9; second volume of, 125; editor of, 9, 10; early friends of, 25; education of, 15, 16, 19-21, 24, 30-32; epitaphs copied by, 106, 107; funeral sermon of John Rogers by, 82; grandfather of, legacy from, 21; joins Newport First Church, 38; Second Church, 60; journey to Springfield, 45-47; to Philadelphia, 115-118; labors at Springfield, 45, 46; in general, 7, 124-126; leaves Second Newport Church, 119; last sickness of, 121, 124; manuscripts of, unpublished, 125; marriages by, in Rehoboth, 122-124; persons baptized by, who were to join Swanzey Church, 124; marriage of, 37; ministry at Swanzey, 33-35; at First Newport, 36; at Second Newport, 60 ff.; at Rehoboth, 120-124; mother's pipe sets house on fire, 94; New Jersey, his visit to, 117; note, supplementary, concerning, 124-126; ordained at Newport, 39; parents of, 15-17; Philadelphia, journey to, 115-118; Philadelphia Association, his accord with, 125; preaches on "Imposition of Hands," 57; prepares for college at Cambridge, 7, 21-30; Providence, visits, 72, 95, 115; receives imposition of hands, 60; reconciliation of, with First Newport Church, 118, 121; Rehoboth, at, 8; removes to, 119; buys a house at, 119; church formed, 120; becomes pastor at, 120; installed, 121; work at, 124; salary of, 43, 48, 57, 58; singing, introduces, at Newport, 58; brief sketch of, 7, 8; small pox, 23, 24; Swanzey, at, 33-35, visits, 95; teaches at Swanzey, 33-35; trouble of, at First Newport Church, 57, 58, 94, 100; his views of doctrine, 7, 8, 125; Wheaton, Rev. Ephraim, his dear friend, 34, 94, 124; wife of, 124, 125; wig, his, 85; wronged by stepfather, 17, 18; Yale College, enters, 7, 30; leaves 7, 33.

Condy, Rev. Jeremiah, 111, 113, 115.
Congregational churches, in R. I., 56.
Counterfeiters, 60-62, 65, 100.
Craft, Ephraim, 26.
Crandall, Rev. Joseph, 108.
Cranston, Gov. Samuel, 48.

Crimes: recorded, 43, 44, 47, 48, 56, 61, 62, 65, 107, 110, 121.

Devotion, John, 46.
Difficulties, church: in First Cong'l Church, Newport, 49-54; in Baptist churches, Swanzey, 35; First Newport, 57, 58, 94, 100, 113, 118; Second Newport, 119.
Drake, Rev. John, 117.
Drunkenness: sexton at Boston guilty of, 112.

Eacclesfield [or, Eaglesfield], Rev. George, 107, 117.
Earthquake, 46.
Episcopalians, practising immersion, 62.
Epitaphs, at Newport, 106, 107.
Everett, Rev. Daniel, 81.
Eyres, Rev. Nicholas, 109, 116.

Fire: at Boston, 16.
Freetown, 110.
Funeral, John Rogers', 82.

Gardner, Capt. Robert, 63 ff.
George II.: proclaimed King, 45.
Gibson, Rev. William, 107.
Green, Dr., of Cambridge, Eng.: strange will of, 113.
Grinman [Greenman] James, 79.

Heat, great, 45.
Hiscox, Rev. William: sermon by, 73; death of, 107.
Holmes, Rev. Obadiah: whipped in Boston, 76.

Inoculation, 22, 23.
Indian War, 32.
Imposition of hands, 7, 8, 40, 57, 78, 92, 94, 125.
Installation, 121.

Jencks, Gov. Joseph, 48.
Jenkins, Rev. N.: letter of, about Henry Loveall, 117.

Laying on of hands: See "Imposition of hands."
Loveall, Henry, 92, 113; bad conduct of, 114, 117, 118.

Mather, Dr. Increase, 19.
Maxwell, Samuel, 63, 65, 66, 77, 78, 108.
Millard, Samuel, 124, 125.
Miller, Gen. Nathan, 125.
Missionary Work, 45, 46.
Mockery: religious service receiving, 108.

Newport: First Baptist Church at, 7, 10, 39, 40, 57, 58, 59; Second Baptist Church of, 7, 40, 119; "Agreement about the meeting house" of, 102-105; Congregational churches of, and their difficulties, 49-54; new meeting house for Mr. Clap, 72.
New Jersey: inquiries concerning the Baptists of, 92.
New York: Dutch church in, 116; sights of, 116.
Note: supplementary, 124-126; concluding words of, 126.

O'Hara, Joseph, 56, 72, 73, 84.
Oldest Baptist Church in America, 10.
Ordination, improper, 117, 118.

Palmer, Rev. Paul, 102, 111, 118.
Peckham, Rev. William, 35.
Peckham, Capt. William, 100.
Pelham, Edward, 111.
Persecution: in Bristol, 62; Baptist petition against, in Connecticut, 79, 80.
Piscataqua (Piscataway), N. J.: Baptist church in, 117.
Providence: Congregational church in, 56.
Potter, Capt. William, 95.

Quakers, 59.
Quarantine, 105, 112.

Rehoboth: Comer goes to, 119; meeting house at, 120; Baptist church of, 120.
Revelation, The: Pardon Tillinghast on, 73-75.
Rhode Island: Counties of, 78; Island of, (Aquidneck), purchase of, 85; settlers adopt constitution for, 86.
Rogers, John, 45; funeral of, 82.
Rogers, Samuel, distress of, 109.
Rogers, Sarah (Mrs. John Comer), 37, 124.
Rogers, Sarah, Mrs. (Mrs. John Comer's mother), death of, 121.
Rogers, William, D. D., 125.

School: first free, in New England, 76.
Seventh Day Baptists, 69, 70.
Sheffield, Nathaniel, 95.
Shipwreck, remarkable, 63-65.
Six-Principle Baptists, 68, 69.
Small pox, 20, 98, 105, 106, 107, 108.
Smith, Edward, 100, 111.
Smith, Philip, 100.
Snow, deep, 121.
Sprague, Rev. Jonathan, 67.
Springfield, Mass.: Baptists at, 45, 46; letter from, 45.
Staples, Thomas, cleared of crime, 105.
Statistics of Baptists in America, 68-70, 85, 114.
Storms, 45, 50, 60.
Sutton, 121.
Swanzey: mentioned, 33; Baptist churches in, 33, 69, 96.
Sweating, Rev. Henry, 49.

Tide, high, at Boston, 26.
Tillinghast, Rev. Pardon: work on The Revelation, 73-75.

Voyage to Boston, 32.
Vincent on the Second Coming of Christ, 20, 21.

Walton, Rev. John, at First Newport Church, 101, 102.
Wheaton, Rev. Ephraim, 34, 44, 94; John Comer's grave by the side of his, 124.
White, Rev. Daniel, 36, 54, 55, 65.
Wightman, Rev. Daniel, baptism by, 109, 110.
Willmarth, Dr. J. W., editorial work of, 10.
Wilson, Rev. John, infamous conduct of, 76.

Yale College: spoken of, 30, 31; Comer enters, 7, 30; leaves, 7, 33.
Year 1727, remarkable, 48.
Year 1730, 114.

INDEX TO FOOT-NOTES.

(Figures refer to numbers of the Foot-notes.)

Adams, Rev. John, 64.
Andover: Congregational churches in, 22.
Andrew, Rev. Samuel, 30.
Angier, Amos, 1.
Antinomians, 62.
Appleton, Nathaniel, D. D., 14.
Apprenticeship, laws of, 4.
Aquidneck: purchase and settlement of, 148, 149, 150.
Aspinwall, William, 155.
Association: Six-Principle Baptist, 102, 123¼, 139.
Authority, of God in the State, 150.

Baker, Rev. Thomas, 118.
Baptist churches: "Calvinistic" in New England, 119, 120, 121.
Baptist churches mentioned: Boston, First, 16, 39, 48; Bristol, Eng., 179; Charleston, S. C. (Somerton), 144; Dartmouth, 110; England, in, 17; Groton, 61, 108; London, Eng. (several), 179; Middletown, 184; New London, 111; Newport (various), 50; Newport, First, 43-45, 56, 65, 66, 91-93, 132, 185¼, 186; Newport, Second, 51, 53, 123¼, 178½; Newport, Seventh Day, 54, 55, 123; Newport, Mr. White's, 56; New York (two), 106, 107; North Carolina, 145; North Kingston, 118; Nottingham, Eng., 179; Piscataqua (Piscataway), 185; Providence (several), 104, 105, 114, 115, 128; Rehoboth, 49, 187, 188; South Kingston, 112, 113; Swanzey (two), 41, 43, 67, 74, 116; Warren, 188; Warwick, 117; Westerly, Seventh Day, 122.
Baptist Principles, Polity and Practice: Arminianism, 106, 107, 119; Associations, 102, 123¼, 139, 187; Church and State, 149, 150, 152; Clarke, Rev. John, 131, 149, 152; communion, 51, 182½; doctrines of grace, 106, 107, 113, 116, 119, 120, 121, 187; elders, 43, 74; helping others, 66; imposition of hands, 51, 91, 141, 187; laying on of hands, *See* "Imposition of Hands"; meeting houses, 123¼, 178½; missionary work, 66, 188; Philadelphia Association, 187; singing in worship, 93, 116; suggestion concerning polity, 75; support of pastors, 128; wicked minister, case of, 183; wine at communion, 182½.
Baptists: church difficulties among, 89, 91, 92, 146, 180, 185½; North Carolina, 145; South Carolina, 144; persecutions of, 16, 39, 42, 97, 105, 109, 131-134, 142, 145, 151, 152, 153-169, 188.
Baker, Rev. Thomas, 118.
Barnard, Rev. John, 23.
Barnes, Rev. Thomas, 116.
Barrows, C. E., D. D.: end of his notes, 187, 188; his views of John Clarke, 152.
Baulstone (or Balstone), William, 166.
Baxter, Rev. Joseph, 79.
Berkeley, Dean George, 95.
Boston: churches in, 18, 19, 20; First Baptist Church of, 39; pastors of First Baptist Church, 39; great fire in, 2.
Boylston, Zabdial, M. D., 11.
Bristol: persecution at, 97.
Brown, Rev. James, 103.
Brown, Rev. Richard, 80.
Browne, Tutor Daniel, 34.
Bull, Henry, 167.
Burnett, Gov. William, 84.

Callender, Rev. Elisha, 16.
Callender, Rev. Ellis, 48.
Callender, Rev. John, 70, 186.
Cambridge, First Congregational Church of, 28.
Canonicut, island of, 85.
Carder, Richard, 165.
Churches: manner of speaking of, 14.
Church and State, 149, 150, 152.
Church polity: Congregationalist, 75; Baptist, *See* "Baptist Principles, Polity and Practice."
Claggett, William, 172.
Clap, Rev. Nathaniel, 25, 77, 83.

INDEX TO FOOT-NOTES. 131

Clap, Rev. Thomas, 69.
Clarke, Rev. James, 52, 178½.
Clarke, Rev. John: spoken of, 44, 131, 152; in accord with regular Baptists, 152; character and work of, 131, 152; Dr. Barrows' views of, 152; "Narrative of," 130.
Clarke, Jeremiah, 178¼.
Comer, John: accord of, with Philadelphia Association, 187; death of, 188; descendants of, 188; difficulties of, with First Church in Newport, 89, 91; labors of, at Sutton and other towns, 188; last days of, 188; his reconciliation with First Church in Newport, 185½; Rehoboth, his usefulness at, 188; sermon on imposition of hands by, 89; his views of doctrine and results, 187.
Coddington, William, 151.
Coggeshall, John, 154.
Communion wine, 182½.
Condy, Rev. Jeremiah, 181; his son Jeremiah, 181.
Congregational churches in Rhode Island, 82, 87.
Constitution adopted by settlers of Aquidneck (island of R. I.), 149, 150.
Cotton, Rev. Josiah, 88.
Council, Congregationalist, at Newport, 81.
Counterfeiting, 96.
Craft, Ephraim, 15.
Crandall, John, 133.
Crandall, Rev. Joseph, 55, 123.
Cranston, Gov. Samuel, 71.
Cutler, Rev. Timothy, 83.
Currency, paper, 13.

Danforth, Samuel, 9.
Dartmouth, church in, 110.
Devotion, Rev Ebenezer, 68.
Difficulties in First Newport Congregational Church, 77, 80, 81, 83.
Drake, Rev. John, 185.
Dyre, William, 161.

Eaglesfield (or, Ecclesfield), Rev. Mr., 184.
Eals (or, Eels), Rev. Nathaniel, 76.
Episcopal church: at Newport, 57, 63; in Providence, 99; at Tower Hill, 100.
Elders in Baptist churches, 43, 74.
Everett, Rev. Daniel, 112.
Eyres, Rev. Nicholas, 106.

Fighting Quaker, 175.
Fire at Boston, 2
Fiske, Rev. Samuel, 115.

Foxcroft, Pres. Thomas, 78.
Freeborn, William, 162.
Free School, first in New England, 135.

General Redemption, 119.
Gibson, Rev. William, 123.
Gifford, Rev. Andrew, 179.
Gorton, Rev. Stephen, 60.
Groton, church in, 108.
Groton Conference, 108.

Hammett, Rev. John, 117.
Hardin, Richard, 67.
Hart, Rev. Oliver, 144.
Hiscox, Rev. William, 123.
Holden, Randall, 168.
Holmes, Rev. Obadiah, 132.
Honeyman, Rev. James, 57, 58.
Hutchinson, William and Anne, 153.
Hutchinson, Edward, 159.

Imposition of hands: in time of Comer, 50, 51, 61, 89, 141, 187; at present time, 187; once general among Baptists in America, 187.
Inoculation, 10, 11.

Jencks, Gov. Joseph, 72.
Jenkins, Rev. Nathaniel, 178.

Laying on of hands: See "Imposition of hands."
Loveall, Henry, 183, 185.

Martin, Rev. Manasseh, 117.
Mason, Rev. Joseph, 116.
Mason, Samuel, 116.
Mather, Dr. Cotton, 3.
Mather, Dr. Increase, 5.
Maxon, Revs. John, John, Jr., and Joseph, 122.
Maxwell, Rev. Samuel, 49, 180.
McSparran, Rev. James, 100.
Middletown, N. J., 184; oldest church in N. J., 184.
Ministers and political affairs, 152.
Modes of punishment, 101.
"Mrs.", meaning of, 46.

New London: church at, 111.
Newport: churches, etc., in, 50, 63; First Baptist Church of, 44, 45, 92, 185½, 186; Second Baptist Church of, 50, 51; deed of its meeting house, 123¼, 178½; Congregational churches in, 24, 63, 73, 77, 80, 81; Seventh Day Baptist Church at, 54, 123;

INDEX TO FOOT-NOTES.

forts at, 137; Mr. Clap's meeting house in, 77, 124; "woods" of, 170.
New York City: Baptist churches in, 107.
North Carolina Baptists, 145.
North Kingston: church in, 118.
Noyes, Rev. Joseph, 27.

O'Hara, Joseph, 123½.
Ordination, 43, 49, 52.

Palmer, Rev. Paul, 146.
Peart, Rev. William, 144.
Peckham, Rev. William, 43.
Pelham, Edward, 182.
Persecutions of Baptists and others: See "Baptists, Persecutions of."
Philadelphia Association: a pattern, 187; doctrinal position of, 187.
Pierpont, Tutor James, 32.
Piggott, Rev. George, 99.
Piscataqua (Piscataway), N. J., spoken of, 185; church in, 185.
Place, Rev. Peter, 114.
Porter, John, 157.
Providence: Congregational church in, 87; division of, and location of churches in, 104, 114, 115, 125.

Quakers spoken of, 59; warlike, 175.

Reconciliation: between John Comer and First Church, Newport, 185½.
Records of Second Church, Newport: extracts from, 123¼.
Rehoboth: Baptist Church at, 187; town of, 188; churches in, 49, 188.
Rhode Island: divided into counties, 138; Indians of, 148.
Rogers, John, 65.

Sanford, John, 158.
Savage, Thomas, 160.
School, free: first in New England, 135.
Screven, Rev. William, 144.
Seventh Day Baptists, 54, 121.
Sever, Rev. Nicholas, 12.
Sheffield, Nathaniel, 173.
Sherman, Philip, 163.
Simmons, Rev. Thomas, 144.
Six-Principle Baptists, 50, 61, 187.

Singing in church, 93.
Slavery and the slave trade, 90.
Small pox, 6.
Smith, Edward, 180.
Smith, Rev. William, 35.
South Carolina Baptists, 144.
South Kingston: church in, 113.
Southworth, Gideon, 37.
Sprague, Rev. Jonathan, 105.
Sprague, Rev. David, 118.
Springfield, Mass.: Baptists at, 66; letter from, 66.
Stennett, Rev. Joseph, 17.
Stocks, the, 101.
Swanzey: town of, 40; Baptist church in, 41; Six-Principle Baptist Church in, 116.
Sweating, Rev. Henry, 74.
Sweet, Rev. Richard, 118.

Tabor, Rev. Philip, 109.
Tillinghast, Rev. Pardon, 128.
Tillinghast, Dea. Pardon, 140.

Usher, Rev. John, 98.

Vincent, Rev. Thomas, 7.

Waldron, Rev. William, 21.
Walker, John, 164.
Walton, Rev. John, 141.
Wanton, Gov. Gideon, 175.
Wanton, John, 169.
Ward, Gov. Richard, 147.
Warwick, church in, 117.
Webb, Rev. John, 8.
Westerly and its churches, 122.
Wheaton, Rev. Ephraim: (Comer's special friend), 41, 42.
White, Rev. Daniel, 45, 56.
Wightman, Rev. Daniel, 53.
Wightman, Rev. Valentine, 61.
Wilbor, Samuel, 156.
Willmarth, Dr. J. W.: Notes and parts of notes by, 14, 42, 46, 75, 94, 123¼, 144, 152, 182½, 183, 187, 188. (Supplementary Note, *pages* 124–126.)
Wilson, Rev. John, 134.
Wine, Communion, 182½.

Yale College, 30, 32.

ABOUT THE AUTHOR

JOHN COMER.
(1704-1734)

To The Editor From David Benedict, D.D., Pawtucket, R.I., May 16, 1859

Dear Sir: My estimate of the character of John Comer is such that I am more than willing to do any thing in my power to honour and perpetuate his memory. In compiling the following sketch, I have access to his well known Diary, which is the principal original source of information concerning him.

JOHN COMER, the eldest son of John and Mary Comer, was born in Boston, Aug. 1st, 1704. His father died at Charleston, S. C., as he was on a voyage to England, to visit his relatives, when John was less than two years of age. He was then left to the care of his mother, and grandfather, of the same name.

The mind of this well disposed youth, according to his own recollections, which go back to his earliest years, was wholly bent on study, merely for the sake of it, and without any particular vocation in view; but, as the family was not in circumstances to support him in his chosen pursuit, at the age of fourteen, he was bound out to a seven years' apprenticeship to learn the glover's trade. For upwards of two years, he submitted quietly to the disposition which his grandfather, who acted as his guardian, had made of him. His master made no complaint of him, except that he "read too much for his business." [1]

Being now in his seventeenth year, by the intercession of Dr. Increase Mather, to whom he applied for his friendly aid, and by the consent of his grandfather, he was released from his apprenticeship, commenced his preparatory studies, and in due time entered the College at Cambridge. His grandfather, dying soon after, left him a legacy of £500. "This," he says, "was to bring me up, and introduce me comfortably in the world, which it did." [2]

After spending some years at Cambridge, —as some of his companions had gone to New Haven, and as living was cheaper there, —by the consent of the Rev. Mr. Webb, who, by his grandfather's will, had become his guardian, he repaired to that institution, where he finished his college course, though I believe he did not graduate on account of ill health. This college then consisted of about fifty students.

Relative to Mr. Comer's experience in the concerns of personal religion, and his change of denominational position, the account may be thus briefly given: His pious propensities in early life have already been stated; but, not relying on the goodness of his morals, or the soundness of his ancestral creed, he sought, and, after a long course of anxious enquiry, obtained, a satisfactory evidence of his conversion, according to what he believed were the scripture requirements. This was at the age of seventeen. In due time, while a member of the College, he united with the Congregational church in Cambridge, then under the pastoral care of the Rev. Nathaniel Appleton. His membership in this church continued about four years, during all which time, he appears to have had much satisfaction with his spiritual home; and all his accounts of his Pastor breathe the spirit of filial affection and

---

[1] In Comer's Diary, I had the following statement: "This year I composed a set Discourse from Eccl. xii. 1—Remember now thy Creator," &c. This was at the age of fifteen, while he was an apprentice; and it evidently shows the bent of his mind at that early age.

[2] Diary, 1721.

About the Author (Continued)

Christian fellowship; and the same may be said, by what appears in his Diary, respecting the other ministers of Boston and elsewhere, who took an interest in his welfare, and of the churches under their care, with which he associated, and occasionally communed.[3]

There was one very alarming event which happened to Boston and vicinity in 1721, just at the time of the serious awakening of young Comer, which served to deepen his religious impressions, and increase his fearful apprehensions of being hurried to his grave, without a due preparation for an exchange of worlds. The small-pox, then the terror of mankind, was making a rapid and, to a great extent, fatal progress, among the people, most of whom had no protection against it. Among the victims of this terrible disease, were some of the most intimate friends of young Comer, whose dread of it was so great, that, according to his own representations, it might be literally said of him, in the language of Young, —

"He felt a thousand deaths in fearing one."

After all his precautions, he was soon seized with the loathsome malady, from the effects of which he barely escaped with his life.[4]

This assiduous enquirer, and very conscientious man, after an investigation of about two years' continuance, adopted the sentiments of the Baptists on the subject and mode of Baptism, and, according to his Diary, was baptized by the Rev. Elisha Callender, January 31, 1725, and united with the First Baptist Church in Boston, of which Mr. C. was then Pastor. Relative to this transaction, in the old journal before me, I find the following entry: — "Having before waited on Rev. Mr. Appleton, of Cambridge, I discoursed with him on the point of Baptism, together with my resolution—upon which he signified that I might, not withstanding, maintain my communion with his church—by which I discovered the candour and catholic spirit of the man. he behaved himself the most like a Christian of any of my friends, at that time, upon that account."[5]

Mr. Comer commenced preaching in 1725, not long after he united with Mr. Callender's church. His first efforts were made with the old Swansea church, which was planted by the famous John Miles, from Wales, in 1668. It was then under the pastoral care of Elder Ephraim Wheaton.[6] Efforts were made to settle the young and promising preacher, as a colleague with

---

[3] These churches, with their Pastors, in 1723, in addition to Cambridge, were, *in Boston*, the Old North, *Cotton Mather*; the New North, *John Webb*; the New Brick, *William Waldron*.

In Andover, John Barnard. In this place young Comer occasionally pursued his classical studies. Andover then was a frontier town.

In Newport, R. I., Nathaniel Clap.

In New Haven, Joseph Noyes.

[4] In the then small population of Boston and vicinity, compared with the present, between eight and nine hundred died of this disease. "The practice of inoculation was *now* set up . . . Dr. Zabdiel Boylston was the chief actor in it—I joined in the *lawfulness* of the practice, though some wrote and printed against it." Comer was preparing to avail himself of the benefit of this new method of prevention, when he found it was too late, and the malady had its natural course. The whole College was dispersed.

[5] Elsewhere Mr. C. remarks that, at this time he knew of no one of his relatives, who was in the Baptist connection.

[6] EPHRAIM WHEATON was an Associate Pastor of this Church as early as 1704; and he continued in the faithful discharge of his duties here until his death, which occurred in 1734, at the age of seventy-five. He lived within the bounds of Rehoboth.

the aged Pastor, but, as the plan failed of success, he repaired to Newport, where, in 1726, he was ordained as Co-pastor with elder William Peckham, in the first church in that town, which bears date, 1644. His ministry here was short but successful; by his influence singing in public worship was there first introduced. He also put in order the old Church Records, which he found in a scattered and neglected condition. The practice of the laying on of hands, (Heb. vi. 2,) as a mode of the initiation of newly baptized members to full fellowship into the church, had hitherto been held in a lax manner, by this ancient community, and Mr. Comer's attempt to have it uniformly observed, was the cause of his dismission from his pastoral charge in 1729. In former ages, this religious rite was a subject of no little discussion and agitation among the Baptists, both in the old country and the new, and sometimes churches were divided on account of differences of opinion respecting it. The Six Principle Baptists, so called, from tenaciously adhering to this number of points laid down in the passage above named, still hold on to this ancient rule of Church Disci-pline. As a general thing, however, the practice has long been disused among the Baptists, both American and foreign.

Mr. Comer preached, as a supply, for nearly two years, in the Second Baptist Church in Newport, which was founded in 1656. It was then under the pastoral care of Elder Daniel Wightman, from whom Mr. Comer received the imposition of hands, in Gospel Order, according to his judgment and belief.

In 1782, this transitory preacher, whose race was rapid and peculiar, and lamentably short, became the Pastor of a church of his own order in the Southern part of old Rehoboth, near to Swansen, and about ten miles from Providence, R. I. Here he died of consumption, May 23, 1734, aged twenty-nine years, nine months and twenty-two days. "He was," says Dr. Jackson, "a gentleman of education, piety, and of great success in his profession. During his brief life, he collected a large body of facts, intending, at some future period, to write the history of the American Baptist Churches. His manuscripts he never printed, nor did he, as I learn, ever prepare them for publication. He was even unable to revise them, and they were, of course, left in their original condition. Nevertheless, he made an able and most valuable contribution to Rhode Island History. His papers were probably written about 1729—1731.[7]

For the historical purposes above named, this industrious man visited most of the churches in New England. He also went as far as Philadelphia; through the Jersies in a Southern direction. He corresponded somewhat extensively for that age, with intelligent men in all the Colonies, where those of this own order could be found, as well as in England, Ireland, and Wales, from which regions many of the earliest emigrants, of the Baptist faith, came to this country. In Comer's time, and at a still later period, Pennsylvania and the Jersies were more distinguished than any of the Colonies for the number of their strong men of this creed. Here were found the Joneses, the Morgans, the Mannings, the Smiths, the Harts, and many others. Could this diligent enquirer have lived to make out the history he proposed, from personal interviews, and from historical documents, then easily obtained, and from

7 Churches in Rhode Island, pp. 80, 81.

reliable traditions, in all the Colonies, where the Society had planted their standards, a great amount of labour would have been saved to the historians who succeeded him.

Comer's Diary, to which reference has already often been made, consists of two thin folio manuscript volumes, of about sixty pages each. Most of them are occupied in the relation of passing events, and in them are found many historical facts concerning the affairs of his own people, and also of all the religious denominations in the land, so far as he had any knowledge of them, or intercourse with them, which appears to have been quite extensive and familiar.

"Comer," says Backus, "was very curious and exact in recording the occurrences of his time." This remark is fully verified by looking over the details of the journal in question. Here we find accounts of earthquakes and storms, of wars and rumours of wars among the Indians at home, and the nations abroad: the doings of the Colonial governments; the names and characters of governmental men, especially of those in the Rhode Island Colony, are often met with in this Diary; and, among other things, is a full account of a petition, which was got up by the ministers and lay-members of the Baptist people, with whom Mr. Comer was associated, against the oppressive laws, which were bearing hard on the few of their brethren, who were scattered "up and down," in the adjoining Colony of Connecticut. The chief matter of complaint in this petition was the perish taxes, for the support of the Standing Order. This document, which is transcribed in full, was endorsed by Governor Jenks, in a respectful note to the Colonial Assembly.

The arrival of the celebrated Dean George Berkeley, at Newport, and some items respecting the popularity of this distinguished visitor, and of the personal interviews which he, in company with others, had with this affable man, are pleasantly related.

Mr. Comer's popularity amongst the ministers and people of different orders is plainly indicated by the frequent entries in his Diary of his correspondence and personal conferences with them. In this way we learn many interesting facts, some painful, some pleasant, respecting men with whom this youthful divine had no ecclesiastical connection. At one time, he informs us that he was invited to the pulpit of the Rev. Mr. Cotton, then the only Congregational clergyman of Providence, which he would gladly have complied with, had not a previous engagement hindered him.

This young minister, during his short race of about nine years after he entered into public service, made his mark unusually high for the time. His name is still had in grateful remembrance in a large religious and literary circle. He left one son and two daughters, and his descendants still survive in Warren, R. I.

Yours respectfully,
DAVID BENEDICT.

William B. Sprague
Annals of the American Pulpit
(New York: Robert Carter & Brothers, 1865)
Volume 6, pages 39-43

THE BAPTIST STANDARD BEARER, INC.
A non-profit, tax-exempt corporation
committed to the Publication & Preservation
of The Baptist Heritage.

SAMPLE TITLES FOR PUBLICATIONS AVAILABLE IN OUR VARIOUS SERIES:

THE BAPTIST *COMMENTARY* SERIES
Sample of authors/works in or near republication:
John Gill - *Exposition of the Old & New Testaments (9 Vol. Set)*
John Gill - *Exposition of Solomon's Song*

THE BAPTIST *FAITH* SERIES:
Sample of authors/works in or near republication:
Abraham Booth - *The Reign of Grace*
John Fawcett - *Christ Precious to Those That Believe*
John Gill - *A Complete Body of Doctrinal & Practical Divinity (2 Vols.)*

THE BAPTIST *HISTORY* SERIES:
Sample of authors/works in or near republication:
Thomas Armitage - *A History of the Baptists (2 Vols.)*
Isaac Backus - *History of the New England Baptists (2 Vols.)*
William Cathcart - *The Baptist Encyclopaedia (3 Vols.)*
J. M. Cramp - *Baptist History*

THE BAPTIST *DISTINCTIVES* SERIES:
Sample of authors/works in or near republication:
Abraham Booth - *Paedobaptism Examined (3 Vols.)*
Alexander Carson - *Ecclesiastical Polity of the New Testament Churches*
E. C. Dargan - *Ecclesiology: A Study of the Churches*
J. M. Frost - *Pedobaptism: Is It From Heaven?*
R. B. C. Howell - *The Evils of Infant Baptism*

THE *DISSENT & NONCONFORMITY* SERIES:
Sample of authors/works in or near republication:
Champlin Burrage - *The Early English Dissenters (2 Vols.)*
Albert H. Newman - *History of Anti-Pedobaptism*
Walter Wilson - *The History & Antiquities of the Dissenting Churches (4 Vols.)*

For a complete list of current authors/titles, visit our internet site at
www.standardbearer.org or write us at:

The Baptist Standard Bearer, Inc.
No. 1 Iron Oaks Drive • Paris, Arkansas 72855

Telephone: (479) 963-3831   Fax: (479) 963-8083
E-mail: baptist@arkansas.net
Internet: http://www.standardbearer.org

Thou hast given a standard to them that fear thee; that it may be displayed because of the truth. -- Psalm 60:4

www.ingramcontent.com/pod-product-compliance
Lightning Source LLC
Chambersburg PA
CBHW032001080426
42735CB00007B/475